NYANSA
CLASSICAL COMMUNITY

YEAR ONE

ELEMENTARY LATIN TEACHER'S GUIDE

Nyansa Classical Community Year One Elementary Latin Teacher's GuideCopyright © 2025 by Nyansa Classical Community

Published in the United States by Nyansa Classical Community

2416 S. Derbigny St.

New Orleans, LA 70125

nyansaclassicalcommunity.org

To order additional materials, please go to www.nyansaclassicalcommunity.org

ISBN 978-1-967443-14-7 (Paperback)
ISBN 978-1-967443-15-4 (eBook)

Cover design by Laura Duffy
Book design by Sarah Scudder
Content developed by Dr. Angel Parham
Latin and English Poetry written by Rebecca Tellinghuisen
Edited by Miriam Asuma and Sophia Scudder

Printed in the United States of America

Credits

Originally developed by Dr. Angel Adams Parham, Co-Founder and Executive Director of Nyansa Classical Community

Formatting and Design by Sarah Scudder

Stories and Poetry written by Rebecca Tellinghuisen

Edited by Miriam Asuma and Sophia Scudder

Images: All images are in the public domain

Acknowledgements

Advanced Studies in Culture Foundation - Charlottesville, VA

Saint John' s College - Annapolis, MD

Introduction

Nyansa's Latin curriculum is designed to provide an introduction to basic Latin vocabulary to students. Each lesson includes Latin vocabulary, a short story using fables, discussion, and games. The curriculum can be used over a four day period, however, the curriculum can be used to fit the schedule of your individual program.

The curriculum works best when students can review the vocabulary words each week. Reviewing the material through flashcards and games will aid your students' memory in learning the vocabulary. The English language uses many Latin roots and parts of words. Gaining an understanding of these roots and parts of words will expand the vocabulary of your students for English. It will build up their language skills, reading skills, and communication.

Each day's lesson will include the following:

- Discussion

- Reading

- Memorization

- Review

Table of Contents

Latin Skills Group

DISCUSS:

Before starting this activity, create cards with the Latin words in the vocabulary bank for this story. You will find these highlighted in the box below. Create a set of one-sided cards with only the Latin terms; another set of one-sided cards with their English meanings; and a third set of cards with the Latin on front and the English on back. This will allow for different kinds of games and reviews. Introduce and discuss the vocabulary words before reading the fable.

Vocabulary Bank	
Canēs	Dog (Canine)
Leonem/Leō	Lion (Leo the constellation)
Vulpēs	Fox
Verum	Truth (verify)
Virtutem	Courage (virtue)
Falsam	FALSE
Victorēs	Victorious (victor, victory)
Pugnāre	Fight (pugnacious)

WEEK ONE: VIRTUE and VICE

Love is caring for a person or thing very much and wishing good towards them.

Hate is disliking a person or thing very much and wishing harm towards them.

The Dogs and the Fox

Illustrator: Harrison Weir, John Tenniel, Ernest Griset, et.al., public domain.

READ:

"The Dogs and the Fox" in English. Use the discussion questions after reading the story aloud.

Some Dogs found the skin of a Lion and furiously began to tear it with their teeth. A Fox chanced to see them and laughed scornfully. If that Lion had been alive," he said, "it would have been a very different story. He would have made you feel how much sharper his claws are than your teeth."

DISCUSS:

Discuss the story using the discussion questions in the guide and/or questions you come up with.

Discussion Questions:
1. What is the message or lesson that you think this fable was trying to tell?
2. What do you think the fox was trying to tell the dogs?
3. What do you think this story is trying to teach?
4. Do you think this story has anything to do with love and hate? If so, what?

MEMORIZE:

Memorize the Latin words from the vocabulary bank using one of the review methods below:

- When working with younger children who are not yet reading fluently (4-6), tell them the Latin word, show it to them, and then ask them to create an action, facial expression, or motion to show what the word means. Once they've come up with these, then show them a Latin card, say the word and their task is to quickly do the action, expression or motion they agreed on. As they get the hang of it, go faster and faster. This helps them to associate the correct English meaning to each corresponding Latin term.

- Younger children will also enjoy the game "Canis, Canis, Lupus". This is played by the same rules as "Duck, Duck, Goose". Canis is Latin for dog and Lupus is Latin for wolf. Since they haven't yet been introduced to the word "lupus", substitute "vulpis"—the word for fox—which is part of today's story.

- When working with older elementary aged children who can read, you can play a card matching game by dividing the students into teams. Feel free to go through several rounds to help them ingrain the words in their memories. Older children (7-11) may also enjoy the more embodied approach described above for younger children.

- The activity Roman Fables in Action is also a good one for both younger and older children. Details for this are in the Year One Teacher's Guide. You can also find them by following the QR code provided at the end of this book.

Latin Skills Group

DISCUSS:

- Ask the children to tell you what they remember from story "The Dogs and the Fox"

- Ask them to put the moral or lesson of the story in their own words. Have the group agree on what this is. Write this down and keep it for future sessions.

- Next, ask the children to help re-write the story in their own words. They should re-tell it in no more than 2-3 sentences. As they experiment aloud with this, you write down what they say, reading it back to them and asking them to help you get the wording right. Write the final summary down and keep it for future sessions.

- Next, tell them that they have all the information they need now to remember and teach the story to someone else. They will do this by memorizing and saying the following: (use the template "Canes et Vulpis".)

Canes et Vulpis

The Dogs and the Fox

The story goes that/One day_____ (insert the 2-3 sentence summary they came up with).

The moral is:_____ (insert the moral they came up with)

MEMORIZE:
Memorize the poem in English. If you're ambitions, you can try to memorize the Latin.

Poem in English
The Dogs and the Fox

The dogs attacked the lion's skin,
but the fox knew the truth,
and he laughed at their false courage.
They were victorious that day,
only because the lion couldn't fight.

Moral: It is easy to feel strong when your enemy has no power.

Poem in Latin
Canes et Vulpis

Canēs pellem leōnis oppugnant,
sed vulpēs verum scit,
et virtutem falsam rīdet.
illo diē sunt victorēs,
solum quod leō pugnāre nōn potest.

Praeceptum: Facile est sentīre sē fortem ubi hostis potestātem nōn habet.

FOLLOW-UP ACTIVITIES:

1. LATIN GAMES

Play some of the Latin games from the Year One Teacher's Guide. You can also find them by following the QR code provided at the end of this book.

2. MATH REVIEW GAMES

For children able to do arithmetic, play number knockout. See Teacher's Guide or use the QR code for more on the Number Knockout game. For younger children, have them choose a number card and then place the correct number of counters by the number. Or, have younger children review number flash cards as high as they can go. Children can be divided into teams for any of these review games.

3. LANGUAGE ARTS REVIEW GAMES

For younger children, divide into teams to identify letter flash cards. Each time a team member gets a card correct the team gets a point. For older children, play spelling bees. Divide into two teams in front of a chalk or white board. Call out the word and whoever

Latin Skills Group

DISCUSS:

- If you did not complete the moral and story re-telling for "The Dogs and the Fox" in your last session, start out by completing it now.

- Next, tell them that they have all the information they need now to remember and teach the story to someone else. They will do this by memorizing and saying the following: (use the template "Canes et Vulpis" found in Day 2.)

- If you did complete it last session, start out by reminding them of the moral and story re-telling they came up with last time and ask them to retell it using the the template "Canes et Vulpis" from Day 2.

MEMORIZE:
Memorize the poem in English. If you're ambitions, you can try to memorize the Latin version, too!

Use English and Latin poem from Day 2.

Learning Through Art

Week One, Day 4 - The Dogs and the Fox

See Learning through Art, Week 1 for instructions.

Latin Skills Group

DISCUSS:

Before starting this activity, create cards with the Latin words in the vocabulary bank for this story. You will find these highlighted in the box below. Create a set of one-sided cards with only the Latin terms; another set of one-sided cards with their English meanings; and a third set of cards with the Latin on front and the English on back. This will allow for different kinds of games and reviews. Introduce and discuss the vocabulary words before reading the fable.

Vocabulary Bank	
Rēx (rēg)	King (regal)
Leo	Lion (the constellation Leo)
Mūris	Mouse
Audit	Hear (audio, auditorium)
Vēnātōrēs	Hunters
Parvum	Small, little
Multis	Many (multiple)
Animalia	Animal, creature
Amīcus	Friend (amicable)

WEEK TWO: VIRTUE and VICE

Compassion is feeling sorry for those who are suffering and wanting to help.

Indifference is ignoring the suffering or needs of others.

The Lion and the Mouse

Milo Winer 1919

READ:

"The Lion and the Mouse" in English. Use the discussion questions after reading the story aloud.

It once happened that a hungry Lion woke to find a Mouse just under his paw. He caught the tiny creature, and was about to make a mouthful of him, when the little fellow looked up, and began to beg for his life.

In most piteous tones the Mouse said: "Do not eat me. I meant no harm coming so near you. If you would only spare my life now, O Lion, I would be sure to repay you!"

The Lion laughed scornfully at this, but it amused him so much that he lifted his paw and let his brave little prisoner go free.

It befell the great Lion, not long afterward, to be in as evil a case as had been the helpless Mouse. And it came about that his life was to be saved by the keeping of the promise he had ridiculed.

He was caught by some hunters, who bound him with a strong rope, while they went away to find means for killing him.

Hearing his loud groans, the Mouse came promptly to his rescue, and gnawed the great rope till the royal captive could set himself free.

"You laughed," the little Mouse said, "at the idea of my being able to be of service to you. You little thought I should repay you. But you see it has come to pass that you are as grateful to me as I was once to you. The weak have their place in the world as truly as the strong."

DISCUSS:
Discuss the story using the discussion questions in the guide and/or questions you come up with.

Discussion Questions:
1. What happened in this story?
2. Did anyone in this story show compassion?
3. Why did the lion scoff when the mouse asked to go free? What kind of attitude does this show us that the Lion had?
4. How was the mouse right in the end?
5. What do you think would have happened if the Lion had chosen not to let the mouse go?

MEMORIZE:

Memorize the Latin words from the vocabulary bank using one of the review methods below:

- When working with younger children who are not yet reading fluently (4-6), tell them the Latin word, show it to them, and then ask them to create an action, facial expression, or motion to show what the word means. Once they've come up with these, then show them a Latin card, say the word and their task is to quickly do the action, expression or motion they agreed on. As they get the hang of it, go faster and faster. This helps them to associate the correct English meaning to each corresponding Latin term.

- Younger children will also enjoy the game "Canis, Canis, Lupus". This is played by the same rules as "Duck, Duck, Goose". Canis is Latin for dog and Lupus is Latin for wolf. Since they haven't yet been introduced to these words, substitute "mus and leo"–the words for mouse and lion–which are part of today's story.

- When working with older elementary aged children who can read, you can play a card matching game by dividing the students into teams. Feel free to go through several rounds to help them ingrain the words in their memories. Older children (7-11) may also enjoy the more embodied approach described above for younger children.

- The activity Roman Fables in Action is also a good one for both younger and older children. Details for this are in the Year One Teacher's Guide. You can also find them by following the QR code provided at the end of this book.

Latin Skills Group

DISCUSS:

- Ask the children to tell you what they remember from story "The Lion and the Mouse"

- Ask them to put the moral or lesson of the story in their own words. Have the group agree on what this is. Write this down and keep it for future sessions.

- Next, ask the children to help re-write the story in their own words. They should re-tell it in no more than 2-3 sentences. As they experiment aloud with this, you write down what they say, reading it back to them and asking them to help you get the wording right. Write the final summary down and keep it for future sessions.

- Next, tell them that they have all the information they need now to remember and teach the story to someone else. They will do this by memorizing and saying the following:

> *Leo et Mus*
>
> *The Lion and the Mouse*
>
> *The story goes that/One day_____ (insert the 2-3 sentence summary they came up with).*
>
> *The moral is:_____ (insert the moral they came up with)*

MEMORIZE:

Memorize the poem in English. If you're ambitions, you can try to memorize the Latin version, too!

Poem in English
The Lion and the Mouse

King of the beasts, the lion laughed
when he heard the mouse's promise.
But when hunters caught him
and bound him tight,
the small creature was indeed his friend.

Moral: A kind deed will be remembered.

Poem in Latin
Leo et Mūs

Rēx bēstiārum, leō rīdet
ubi prōmissum mūris audit.
Sed ubi vēnātōrēs eum capiunt
et artē eum ligant,
parvum animal verē est amīcus.

Praeceptum: Factum benignum memoriā tenēbitur.

FOLLOW-UP ACTIVITIES:

1. LATIN GAMES

Play some of the Latin games. Details for this are in the Year One Teacher's Guide. You can also find them by following the QR code provided at the end of this book.

2. MATH REVIEW GAMES

For children able to do arithmetic, play number knockout. See the Teacher's Guide or QR code for more on the Number Knockout game. For younger children, have them choose a number card and then place the correct number of counters by the number. Or, have younger children review number flash cards as high as they can go. Children can be divided into teams for any of these review games.

3. LANGUAGE ARTS REVIEW GAMES

For younger children, divide into teams to identify letter flash cards. Each time a team member gets a card correct the team gets a point. For older children, play spelling bees. Divide into two teams in front of a chalk or white board. Call out the word and whoever

Latin Skills Group

DISCUSS:

- If you did not complete the moral and story re-telling for "The Lion and the Mouse" in your last session, start out by completing it now.

- Next, tell them that they have all the information they need now to remember and teach the story to someone else. They will do this by memorizing and saying the following: (use the template "Leo et Mus" found in Day 2.)

- If you did complete it last session, start out by reminding them of the moral and story re-telling they came up with last time and ask them to retell it using the template of "Leo et Mus."

MEMORIZE:
Memorize the poem in English. If you're ambitions, you can try to memorize the Latin version, too!

Use English and Latin poem from Day 2.

Learning Through Art

Week Two, Day 4 - The Lion and the Mouse

See Learning through Art, Week 2 for instructions.

Latin Skills Group

DISCUSS:

Before starting this activity, create cards with the Latin words in the vocabulary bank for this story. You will find these highlighted in the box below. Create a set of one-sided cards with only the Latin terms; another set of one-sided cards with their English meanings; and a third set of cards with the Latin on front and the English on back. This will allow for different kinds of games and reviews. Introduce and discuss the vocabulary words before reading the fable.

Vocabulary Bank	
Asinus	Donkey (ass)
Vulpēs	Fox
Amīcī	Friends (amity)
Leō	Lion (leonine)
Appāret	Appears (apparition)
Servāre	Save
Miserum	Poor, wretched (miserable)
Dūcit (ducere)	Leads (duct, conduct)
Esuriens	Hungry
Prīmum	First (primary)

WEEK TWO: VIRTUE and VICE

Forgiveness is not holding someone else's bad actions against them.

Vengeance is trying to make someone suffer because of their actions towards you.

The Donkey, the Fox and the Lion

Milo Winter 1919

READ:

"The Donkey, the Fox, and the Lion" in English. Use the discussion questions after reading the story aloud.

A Donkey and a Fox had become close comrades, and were constantly in each other's company. While the Donkey cropped a fresh bit of greens, the Fox would devour a chicken from the neighboring farmyard or a bit of cheese filched from the dairy. One day the pair unexpectedly met a Lion. The Donkey was very much frightened, but the Fox calmed his fears.

"I will talk to him," he said.

So the Fox walked boldly up to the Lion.

"Your highness," he said in an undertone, so the Donkey could not hear him, "I've got a fine scheme in my head. If you promise not to hurt me, I will lead that foolish creature yonder into a pit where he can't get out, and you can feast at your pleasure."

The Lion agreed and the Fox returned to the Donkey.

"I made him promise not to hurt us," said the Fox. "But come, I know a good place to hide till he is gone."

So the Fox led the Donkey into a deep pit. But when the Lion saw that the Donkey was his for the taking, he first of all struck down the traitor Fox.

DISCUSS:

Discuss the story using the discussion questions in the guide and/or questions you come up with.

Discussion Questions:
1. What happened in this story?
2. Why do you think the lion killed the fox anyway?
3. Can you think of any other way that the donkey and fox could have escaped from the lion without the fox betraying his friend?
4. Did anyone in this story behave in a way that you think you should copy?

MEMORIZE:

Memorize the Latin words from the vocabulary bank using one of the review methods below:

- When working with younger children who are not yet reading fluently (4-6), tell them the Latin word, show it to them, and then ask them to create an action, facial expression, or motion to show what the word means. Once they've come up with these, then show them a Latin card, say the word and their task is to quickly do the action, expression or motion they agreed on. As they get the hang of it, go faster and faster. This helps them to associate the correct English meaning to each corresponding Latin term.

- Younger children will also enjoy the game "Canis, Canis, Lupus". This is played by the same rules as "Duck, Duck, Goose". Canis is Latin for dog and Lupus is Latin for wolf. Since they haven't yet been introduced to these words, substitute "asinus, vulpis, or leo"–the words for donkey, fox, and lion–which are part of today's story.

- When working with older elementary aged children who can read, you can play a card matching game by dividing the students into teams. Feel free to go through several rounds to help them ingrain the words in their memories. Older children (7-11) may also enjoy the more embodied approach described above for younger children.

Latin Skills Group

DISCUSS:

- Ask the children to tell you what they remember from story "The Donkey, the Fox and the Lion"

- Ask them to put the moral or lesson of the story in their own words. Have the group agree on what this is. Write this down and keep it for future sessions.

- Next, ask the children to help rewrite the story in their own words. They should re-tell it in no more than 2-3 sentences. As they experiment aloud with this, you write down what they say, reading it back to them and asking them to help you get the wording right. Write the final summary down and keep it for future sessions.

- Next, tell them that they have all the information they need now to remember and teach the story to someone else. They will do this by memorizing and saying the following:

> *Asinus, Vulpis, et Leo*
>
> *The Donkey, the Fox and the Lion*
>
> *The story goes that/One day_____ (insert the 2-3 sentence summary they came up with).*
>
> *The moral is:_____ (insert the moral they came up with)*

Memorize:

Memorize the poem in English. If you're ambitions, you can try to memorize the Latin version, too!

Poem in English

The Donkey, the Fox, and the Lion

Donkey and fox were once friends,
then the lion appeared.
Fox wanted to save himself
and led the poor donkey into a pit.
But the lion, still hungry, took the betrayer first.

Moral: He who betrays a friend often falls into his own trap.

Poem in Latin

Asinus, Vulpis, et Leo

Ōlim asinus et vulpēs sunt amīcī,
tunc leō appāret.
Vulpēs sē servāre cupit
et in foveam asinum miserum dūcit.
Sed leō, etiam esuriens, prōditōrem prīmum capit.

Praeceptum: Quī amīcum prōdidit saepe in laqueum suum incidit.

FOLLOW-UP ACTIVITIES:

1. LATIN GAMES

Play some of the Latin games from the Year One Teacher's Guide. You can also find them by following the QR code provided at the end of this book..

2. MATH REVIEW GAMES

For children able to do arithmetic, play number knockout. See the Teacher's Guide or QR code for more on the Number Knockout game. For younger children, have them choose a number card and then place the correct number of counters by the number. Or, have younger children review number flash cards as high as they can go. Children can be divided into teams for any of these review games.

3. LANGUAGE ARTS REVIEW GAMES

For younger children, divide into teams to identify letter flash cards. Each time a team member gets a card correct the team gets a point. For older children, play spelling bees. Divide into two teams in front of a chalk or white board. Call out the word and whoever

Latin Skills Group

DISCUSS:

- If you did not complete the moral and story re-telling for "The Donkey, the Fox and the Lion" in your last session, start out by completing it now.

- Next, tell them that they have all the information they need now to remember and teach the story to someone else. They will do this by memorizing and saying the following: (use the template "Asinus, Vulpis, et Leo" found in Day 2.)

- If you did complete it last session, start out by reminding them of the moral and story re-telling they came up with last time and ask them to retell it using the template of "Asinus, Vulpis, et Leo" found in Day 2.

MEMORIZE:
Memorize the poem in English. If you're ambitions, you can try to memorize the Latin version, too!

Use English and Latin poem from Day 2.

Learning Through Art

Week Three, Day 4 - The Donkey, the Fox, and the Lion

See Learning through Art, Week 3 for instructions.

Latin Skills Group

DISCUSS:

Before starting this activity, create cards with the Latin words in the vocabulary bank for this story. You will find these highlighted in the box below. Create a set of one-sided cards with only the Latin terms; another set of one-sided cards with their English meanings; and a third set of cards with the Latin on front and the English on back. This will allow for different kinds of games and reviews. Introduce and discuss the vocabulary words before reading the fable.

Vocabulary Bank	
Leō	Lion
Fortis	Strong (fortitude)
Pulcher	Beautiful (pulchrify)
Vetus	Old (veteran)
Cōnsūmere	Eat (consume)
Aper	Boar
Taurus	Bull (constellation Taurus)
Asinus	Donkey
Timent	Fear (timid)
Priorem	Former (prior)

WEEK TWO: VIRTUE and VICE

Kindness is treating others with respect, gentleness, and compassion.

Cruelty is hurting others on purpose.

The Old Lion

C. Whittingham (1814)

READ:

"The Old Lion" in English. Use the discussion questions after reading the story aloud.

A Lion had grown very old. His teeth were worn away. His limbs could no longer bear him, and the King of Beasts was very pitiful indeed as he lay gasping on the ground, about to die.

Where now is his strength and his former graceful beauty?

Now a Boar spied him, and rushing at him, gored him with his yellow tusk. A Bull trampled him with his heavy hoofs. Even a contemptible Ass let fly his heels and brayed his insults in the face of the Lion.

DISCUSS:

Discuss the story using the discussion questions in the guide and/or questions you come up with.

Discussion Questions:

1. What happened in this story?
2. Why do you think the other animals treated the lion this way?
3. Do you think that those animals behaved in the way they should have?
4. If you were one of these animals, what do you think you would have done?
5. Our virtue this week is kindness. Did anyone show kindness in this story?
6. Who can tell this story again, but this time change it to make the animals kind?

MEMORIZE:

Memorize the Latin words from the vocabulary bank using one of the review methods below:

- When working with younger children who are not yet reading fluently (4-6), tell them the Latin word, show it to them, and then ask them to create an action, facial expression, or motion to show what the word means. Once they've come up with these, then show them a Latin card, say the word and their task is to quickly do the action, expression or motion they agreed on. As they get the hang of it, go faster and faster. This helps them to associate the correct English meaning to each corresponding Latin term.

- Younger children will also enjoy the game "Canis, Canis, Lupus". This is played by the same rules as "Duck, Duck, Goose". Canis is Latin for dog and Lupus is Latin for wolf. Since they haven't yet been introduced to these words, substitute "taurus and leo"–the words for bull and lion–which are part of today's story.

- When working with older elementary aged children who can read, you can play a card matching game by dividing the students into teams. Feel free to go through several rounds to help them ingrain the words in their memories. Older children (7-11) may also enjoy the more embodied approach described above for younger children.

- The activity Roman Fables in Action is also a good one for both younger and older children. Details for this are in the Year One Teacher's Guide. You can also find them by following the QR code provided at the end of this book.

Latin Skills Group

DISCUSS:

- Ask the children to tell you what they remember from story "The Old Lion"

- Ask them to put the moral or lesson of the story in their own words. Have the group agree on what this is. Write this down and keep it for future sessions.

- Next, ask the children to help rewrite the story in their own words. They should re-tell it in no more than 2-3 sentences. As they experiment aloud with this, you write down what they say, reading it back to them and asking them to help you get the wording right. Write the final summary down and keep it for future sessions.

- Next, tell them that they have all the information they need now to remember and teach the story to someone else. They will do this by memorizing and saying the following:

> *Leo Vetus*
>
> *The Old Lion*
>
> *The story goes that/One day_____ (insert the 2-3 sentence summary they came up with).*
>
> *The moral is:_____ (insert the moral they came up with)*

Memorize:

Memorize the poem in English. If you're ambitions, you can try to memorize the Latin version, too!

The Old Lion

Once the lion had been beautiful and strong,
but he was old and could not eat or move.
The boar, bull, and ass feared him before,
But now, instead of running away,
they attacked and mocked the former king.

Moral: It is cruel to mock those who have fallen.

Poem in Latin

Leo Vetus

Ōlim leō erat pulcher et fortis,
sed nunc vetus, cōnsūmere aut movēre nōn potest.
Aper, taurus, et asinus antea eum timent,
sed nunc, nōn currunt.
Rēgem priorem oppugnant et dērīdent.

Praeceptum: Crūdēle est irrīdēre illōs quī cecidērunt.

FOLLOW-UP ACTIVITIES:

1. LATIN GAMES

Play some of the Latin games from the Year One Teacher's Guide or QR code at the end of the book.

2. MATH REVIEW GAMES

For children able to do arithmetic, play number knockout. See the Teacher's Guide or QR code for more on the Number Knockout game. For younger children, have them choose a number card and then place the correct number of counters by the number. Or, have younger children review number flash cards as high as they can go. Children can be divided into teams for any of these review games.

3. LANGUAGE ARTS REVIEW GAMES

For younger children, divide into teams to identify letter flash cards. Each time a team member gets a card correct the team gets a point. For older children, play spelling bees. Divide into two teams in front of a chalk or white board. Call out the word and whoever spells it fastest and correctly gets a point for their team.

Latin Skills Group

DISCUSS:

- If you did not complete the moral and story retelling for "The Old Lion" in your last session, start out by completing it now.

- Next, tell them that they have all the information they need now to remember and teach the story to someone else. They will do this by memorizing and saying the following: Use the template from Day 2.

- If you did complete it last session, start out by reminding them of the moral and story re-telling they came up with last time and ask them to retell it using the formula above. Use the template from Day 2.

MEMORIZE:
Memorize the poem in English. If you're ambitions, you can try to memorize the Latin version, too!

Use English and Latin poem from Day 2.

Learning Through Art

Week Four, Day 4 - The Old Lion

See Learning through Art, Week 4 for instructions.

Latin Skills Group

DISCUSS:

Before starting this activity, create cards with the Latin words in the vocabulary bank for this story. You will find these highlighted in the box below. Create a set of one-sided cards with only the Latin terms; another set of one-sided cards with their English meanings; and a third set of cards with the Latin on front and the English on back. This will allow for different kinds of games and reviews. Introduce and discuss the vocabulary words before reading the fable.

Vocabulary Bank	
Asinus	Donkey
Lupus	Wolf
Advenientem	Come (advent)
Videt	See (video)
Cōnsilium	Plan (counsel, council)
Pedem	Foot (pedestrian)
Īnspicit	Inspects
Spinam	Thorn (spine)
Sentit	Feels (sensation)
Ēvādit	Gets away, escapes (evade)

WEEK FIVE: VIRTUE and VICE

Humility is acknowledging your own flaws and recognizing the gifts of others.

Arrogance is thinking you are much better than other people.

The Donkey and the Wolf

Milo Winter 1919

READ:

"The Donkey and the Wolf" in English. Use the discussion questions after reading the story aloud.

A Donkey was feeding in a pasture near a wood when he saw a Wolf lurking in the shadows along the hedge. He easily guessed what the Wolf had in mind, and thought of a plan to save himself. So he pretended he was lame, and began to hobble painfully.

When the Wolf came up, he asked the Donkey what had made him lame, and the Donkey replied that he had stepped on a sharp thorn.

"Please pull it out," he pleaded, groaning as if in pain. "If you do not, it might stick in your throat when you eat me."

The Wolf saw the wisdom of the advice, for he wanted to enjoy his meal without any danger of choking. So the Donkey lifted up his foot and the Wolf began to search very closely and carefully for the thorn.

Just then the Donkey kicked out with all his might, tumbling the Wolf a dozen paces away. And while the Wolf was getting very slowly and painfully to his feet, the Donkey galloped away in safety.

"Serves me right," growled the Wolf as he crept into the bushes. "I'm a butcher by trade, not a doctor."

DISCUSS:

Discuss the story using the discussion questions in the guide and/or questions you come up with.

Discussion Questions:
1. What happened in this story?
2. Do you think what the donkey did was right or wrong? What about the wolf?
3. Note: There is no specific correct answer to this question. Its purpose is to engender dialogue, not to absolutely determine the justice of either animal's behavior.
4. What lesson do you think this story might be trying to teach?
5. Our virtue this week is humility. Did anyone in this story show or learn humility?

MEMORIZE:

Memorize the Latin words from the vocabulary bank using one of the review methods below:

- When working with younger children who are not yet reading fluently (4-6), tell them the Latin word, show it to them, and then ask them to create an action, facial expression, or motion to show what the word means. Once they've come up with these, then show them a Latin card, say the word and their task is to quickly do the action, expression or motion they agreed on. As they get the hang of it, go faster and faster. This helps them to associate the correct English meaning to each corresponding Latin term.

- Younger children will also enjoy the game "Canis, Canis, Lupus". This is played by the same rules as "Duck, Duck, Goose". Canis is Latin for dog and Lupus is Latin for wolf. Since they haven't yet been introduced to "canis", substitute "asinus"–the word for donkey–which is part of today's story.

- When working with older elementary aged children who can read, you can play a card matching game by dividing the students into teams. Feel free to go through several rounds to help them ingrain the words in their memories. Older children (7-11) may also enjoy the more embodied approach described above for younger children.

Latin Skills Group

DISCUSS:

- Ask the children to tell you what they remember from story "The Donkey and the Wolf"

- Ask them to put the moral or lesson of the story in their own words. Have the group agree on what this is. Write this down and keep it for future sessions.

- Next, ask the children to help rewrite the story in their own words. They should re-tell it in no more than 2-3 sentences. As they experiment aloud with this, you write down what they say, reading it back to them and asking them to help you get the wording right. Write the final summary down and keep it for future sessions.

- Next, tell them that they have all the information they need now to remember and teach the story to someone else. They will do this by memorizing and saying the following:

> *Asinus et Lupus*
>
> *The Donkey and the Wolf*
>
> *The story goes that/One day_____ (insert the 2-3 sentence summary they came up with).*
>
> *The moral is:_____ (insert the moral they came up with)*

Memorize:

Memorize the poem in English. If you're ambitions, you can try to memorize the Latin version, too!

Poem in English

The Donkey and the Wolf

Donkey saw the wolf approaching
and made a plan: "I'll be lame."
When the wolf inspected donkey's foot,
he didn't find a thorn—but felt a kick!
And the donkey got away.

Moral: One who acts falsely often fails to recognize another liar.

Poem in Latin

Asinus et Lupus

Asinus lupum advenientem videt
et cōnsilium capit: "Claudus ero."
Ubi lupus pedem asinī īnspicit,
spīnam nōn invenit—sed calcem sentit!
Et asinus ēvādit.

Praeceptum: Quī falsē agit saepe alium mendācem nōn agnōscit.

FOLLOW-UP ACTIVITIES:

1. LATIN GAMES
Play some of the Latin games from the Year One Teacher's Guide or QR code.

2. MATH REVIEW GAMES
For children able to do arithmetic, play number knockout. See the Year One Teacher's Guide or QR code for more on the Number Knockout game. For younger children, have them choose a number card and then place the correct number of counters by the number. Or, have younger children review number flash cards as high as they can go. Children can be divided into teams for any of these review games.

3. LANGUAGE ARTS REVIEW GAMES
For younger children, divide into teams to identify letter flash cards. Each time a team member gets a card correct the team gets a point. For older children, play spelling bees. Divide into two teams in front of a chalk or white board. Call out the word and whoever spells it fastest and correctly gets a point for their team.

Latin Skills Group

DISCUSS:

- If you did not complete the moral and story re-telling for "The Donkey and the Wolf" in your last session, start out by completing it now.

- Next, tell them that they have all the information they need now to remember and teach the story to someone else. They will do this by memorizing and saying the following: use the template from Day 2.

- If you did complete it last session, start out by reminding them of the moral and story re-telling they came up with last time and ask them to retell it using the formula above. Use the template from Day 2.

MEMORIZE:

Memorize the poem in English. If you're ambitions, you can try to memorize the Latin version, too!

Use English and Latin poem from Day 2.

Learning Through Art

Week Five, Day 4 - The Donkey and the Wolf

See Learning through Art, Week 5 for instructions.

Latin Skills Group

DISCUSS:

Before starting this activity, create cards with the Latin words in the vocabulary bank for this story. You will find these highlighted in the box below. Create a set of one-sided cards with only the Latin terms; another set of one-sided cards with their English meanings; and a third set of cards with the Latin on front and the English on back. This will allow for different kinds of games and reviews. Introduce and discuss the vocabulary words before reading the fable.

Vocabulary Bank	
Leo	Lion
Vetus	Old (veteran)
Capere	Catch, seize (capture)
Cavernam	Cave, cavern
Manet	Stays, remains (mansion)
Vīcīnēs	Neighbors (vicinity)
Vīsitant	Visit (visitation)
Vulpēs	Fox
Vestīgia	Steps, tracks (investigate, vestige)
Videt	Sees (video)
Sapienter	Wisely (homo sapiens)
Invītātiōnem	Invitation

WEEK SIX: VIRTUE and VICE

Wisdom is knowing the right thing to do in every different situation.

Foolishness is making bad decisions and ignoring good advice.

The Old Lion and the Fox

Milo Winter 1919

READ:

"The Old Lion and the Fox" in English. Use the discussion questions after reading the story aloud.

An old Lion, whose teeth and claws were so worn that it was not so easy for him to get food as in his younger days, pretended that he was sick. He took care to let all his neighbors know about it, and then lay down in his cave to wait for visitors. And when they came to offer him their sympathy, he ate them up one by one.

The Fox came too, but he was very cautious about it. Standing at a safe distance from the cave, he inquired politely after the Lion's health. The Lion replied that he was very ill indeed, and asked the Fox to step in for a moment. But Master Fox very wisely stayed outside, thanking the Lion very kindly for the invitation.

"I should be glad to do as you ask," he added, "but I have noticed that there are many footprints leading into your cave and none coming out. Pray tell me, how do your visitors find their way out again?"

DISCUSS:

Discuss the story using the discussion questions in the guide and/or questions you come up with.

Discussion Questions:
1. What happened in this story?
2. Why did the Lion tell the neighbors he was sick? Was he actually sick?
3. Why do you think the fox didn't go into the cave?
4. Did anyone in this story show wisdom? How?
5. What do you think would have happened if the fox had not noticed the footprints?

MEMORIZE:

Memorize the Latin words from the vocabulary bank using one of the review methods below:

- When working with younger children who are not yet reading fluently (4-6), tell them the Latin word, show it to them, and then ask them to create an action, facial expression, or motion to show what the word means. Once they've come up with these, then show them a Latin card, say the word and their task is to quickly do the action, expression or motion they agreed on. As they get the hang of it, go faster and faster. This helps them to associate the correct English meaning to each corresponding Latin term.

- Younger children will also enjoy the game "Canis, Canis, Lupus". This is played by the same rules as "Duck, Duck, Goose". Canis is Latin for dog and Lupus is Latin for wolf. Since they haven't yet been introduced to these words, substitute "vulpes and leo"—the words for fox and lion—which are part of today's story.

- When working with older elementary aged children who can read, you can play a card matching game by dividing the students into teams. Feel free to go through several rounds to help them ingrain the words in their memories. Older children (7-11) may also enjoy the more embodied approach described above for younger children.

- The activity Roman Fables in Action is also a good one for both younger and older children. Details for this are in the Year One Teacher's Guide. You can also find them by following the QR code provided at the end of this book.

Latin Skills Group

DISCUSS:

- Ask the children to tell you what they remember from story "The Old Lion and the Fox"

- Ask them to put the moral or lesson of the story in their own words. Have the group agree on what this is. Write this down and keep it for future sessions.

- Next, ask the children to help rewrite the story in their own words. They should re-tell it in no more than 2-3 sentences. As they experiment aloud with this, you write down what they say, reading it back to them and asking them to help you get the wording right. Write the final summary down and keep it for future sessions.

- Next, tell them that they have all the information they need now to remember and teach the story to someone else. They will do this by memorizing and saying the following:

Leo et Vulpes

The Old Lion and the Fox

The story goes that/One day_____ (insert the 2-3 sentence summary they came up with).

The moral is:_____ (insert the moral they came up with)

Memorize:

Memorize the poem in English. If you're ambitions, you can try to memorize the Latin version, too!

Poem in English

The Old Lion and the Fox

An old lion could not catch food,
so he stayed in his cave, pretending to be sick.
Neighbors visited him, but they did not leave.
When the fox noticed tracks in one direction only,
he wisely refused the lion's invitation.

Moral: Sharp eyes will discover false words.

Poem in Latin

Leo et Vulpes

Leō vetus capere nōn potest,
ita in cavernam manet, fingens morbum.
Vīcīnēs eum vīsitant, sed nōn dēcēdunt.
Ubi vulpēs vestīgia solum in unā parte animadvertit,
invītātiōnem leōnis sapienter recūsat.

Praeceptum: Oculī ācrēs verba falsa inveniet.

FOLLOW-UP ACTIVITIES:

1. LATIN GAMES
Play some of the Latin games from the Year One Teacher's Guide or QR code at the end of the book. .

2. MATH REVIEW GAMES
For children able to do arithmetic, play number knockout. See the Year One Teacher's Guide or QR code for more on the Number Knockout game. For younger children, have them choose a number card and then place the correct number of counters by the number. Or, have younger children review number flash cards as high as they can go. Children can be divided into teams for any of these review games.

3. LANGUAGE ARTS REVIEW GAMES
For younger children, divide into teams to identify letter flash cards. Each time a team member gets a card correct the team gets a point. For older children, play spelling bees. Divide into two teams in front of a chalk or white board. Call out the word and whoever spells it fastest and correctly gets a point for their team.

Latin Skills Group

DISCUSS:

- If you did not complete the moral and story re-telling for "The Old Lion and the Fox" in your last session, start out by completing it now.

- Next, tell them that they have all the information they need now to remember and teach the story to someone else. They will do this by memorizing and saying the following: use the template from Day 2.

- If you did complete it last session, start out by reminding them of the moral and story re-telling they came up with last time and ask them to retell it using the formula above. Use the template from Day 2.

MEMORIZE:

Memorize the poem in English. If you're ambitions, you can try to memorize the Latin version, too!

Use English and Latin poem from Day 2.

Learning Through Art

Week Six, Day 4 - The Old Lion and the Fox

See Learning through Art, Week 6 for instructions.

Latin Skills Group

DISCUSS:

Before starting this activity, create cards with the Latin words in the vocabulary bank for this story. You will find these highlighted in the box below. Create a set of one-sided cards with only the Latin terms; another set of one-sided cards with their English meanings; and a third set of cards with the Latin on front and the English on back. This will allow for different kinds of games and reviews. Introduce and discuss the vocabulary words before reading the fable.

Vocabulary Bank	
Lupus	Wolf
Agnum	Lamb
Aufert	Carries away (ferry)
Dēsīderat	Wants (desire)
Leō	Lion
Murmurat	Complains (murmur)
Dīcit (dicere)	Says (dictate, dictionary)
Recordāre	Recall (record)

WEEK SEVEN: VIRTUE and VICE

Justice is giving to each person what they deserve.

Injustice is keeping from others what rightfully belongs to them.

The Wolf and the Lion

Milo Winter 1919

READ:

"The Wolf and the Lion" in English. Use the discussion questions after reading the story aloud.

A Wolf had stolen a Lamb and was carrying it off to his lair to eat it. But his plans were very much changed when he met a Lion, who, without making any excuses, took the Lamb away from him.

The Wolf made off to a safe distance, and then said in a much injured tone:

"You have no right to take my property like that!"

The Lion looked back, but as the Wolf was too far away to be taught a lesson without too much inconvenience, he said:

"Your property? Did you buy it, or did the Shepherd make you a gift of it? Pray tell me, how did you get it?"

DISCUSS:

Discuss the story using the discussion questions in the guide and/or questions you come up with.

Discussion Questions:

1. What happened in this story?
2. How had the wolf gotten the sheep?
3. Was that a just or right way of getting what he wanted?
4. What happened to him as a result?
5. Somebody in the story told us two better options for getting something we want or need. Can anyone remember what those other two options were and who suggested them?

MEMORIZE:

Memorize the Latin words from the vocabulary bank using one of the review methods below:

- When working with younger children who are not yet reading fluently (4-6), tell them the Latin word, show it to them, and then ask them to create an action, facial expression, or motion to show what the word means. Once they've come up with these, then show them a Latin card, say the word and their task is to quickly do the action, expression or motion they agreed on. As they get the hang of it, go faster and faster. This helps them to associate the correct English meaning to each corresponding Latin term.

- Younger children will also enjoy the game "Canis, Canis, Lupus". This is played by the same rules as "Duck, Duck, Goose". Canis is Latin for dog and Lupus is Latin for wolf. Since they haven't yet been introduced to these words, substitute "leo and lupus"–the words for lion and wolf–which are part of today's story.

- When working with older elementary aged children who can read, you can play a card matching game by dividing the students into teams. Feel free to go through several rounds to help them ingrain the words in their memories. Older children (7-11) may also enjoy the more embodied approach described above for younger children.

- The activity Roman Fables in Action is also a good one for both younger and older children. Details for this are in the Year One Teacher's Guide. You can also find them by following the QR code provided at the end of this book.

Latin Skills Group

DISCUSS:

- Ask the children to tell you what they remember from story "The Wolf and the Lion"

- Ask them to put the moral or lesson of the story in their own words. Have the group agree on what this is. Write this down and keep it for future sessions.

- Next, ask the children to help re-write the story in their own words. They should re-tell it in no more than 2-3 sentences. As they experiment aloud with this, you write down what they say, reading it back to them and asking them to help you get the wording right. Write the final summary down and keep it for future sessions.

- Next, tell them that they have all the information they need now to remember and teach the story to someone else. They will do this by memorizing and saying the following:

> *Lupus et Leo*
>
> *The Wolf and the Lion*
>
> *The story goes that/One day_____ (insert the 2-3 sentence summary they came up with).*
>
> *The moral is:_____ (insert the moral they came up with)*

Memorize:

Memorize the poem in English. If you're ambitions, you can try to memorize the Latin version, too!

Poem in English

The Wolf and the Lion

A wolf snatched a lamb
and was carrying it away,
but the lion wanted it too.
When the wolf complained, the lion said,
"Recall—you were the first thief."

Moral: Do not cry when the thing you stole is stolen.

Poem in Latin

Lupus et Leo

Lupus agnum capit
et eum aufert,
sed leō eum dēsīderat quoque.
Ubi lupus murmurat, leō dīcit,
"Recordāre—tū est prīmus fūr."

Praeceptum: Nōlī lacrimāre ubi rēs quam abstulistī aufertur.

FOLLOW-UP ACTIVITIES:

1. LATIN GAMES

Play some of the Latin games from the Year One Teacher's Guide or QR code at the end of the book. .

2. MATH REVIEW GAMES

For children able to do arithmetic, play number knockout. See the Teacher's Guide or QR code for more on the Number Knockout game. For younger children, have them choose a number card and then place the correct number of counters by the number. Or, have younger children review number flash cards as high as they can go. Children can be divided into teams for any of these review games.

3. LANGUAGE ARTS REVIEW GAMES

For younger children, divide into teams to identify letter flash cards. Each time a team member gets a card correct the team gets a point. For older children, play spelling bees. Divide into two teams in front of a chalk or white board. Call out the word and whoever spells it fastest and correctly gets a point for their team.

Latin Skills Group

DISCUSS:

- If you did not complete the moral and story re-telling for "The Wolf and the Lion" in your last session, start out by completing it now.

- Next, tell them that they have all the information they need now to remember and teach the story to someone else. They will do this by memorizing and saying the following: use the template from Day 2.

- If you did complete it last session, start out by reminding them of the moral and story re-telling they came up with last time and ask them to retell it using the formula above. Use the template from Day 2.

MEMORIZE:

Memorize the poem in English. If you're ambitions, you can try to memorize the Latin version, too!

Use English and Latin poem from Day 2.

Learning Through Art

Week Seven, Day 4 - The Old Lion and the Fox

See Learning through Art, Week 7 for instructions.

Latin Skills Group

DISCUSS:

Before starting this activity, create cards with the Latin words in the vocabulary bank for this story. You will find these highlighted in the box below. Create a set of one-sided cards with only the Latin terms; another set of one-sided cards with their English meanings; and a third set of cards with the Latin on front and the English on back. This will allow for different kinds of games and reviews. Introduce and discuss the vocabulary words before reading the fable.

Vocabulary Bank	
Lupus	Wolf
Canis	Dog
Convenit	Meets (convention)
Speciē	Appearance (species)
Sententiam dīxit	Commented (sentence)
Vitam	Life (vital, vitamin)
Laudat	Praises (laud)
Putat	Thinks (computer)
Grandem	Grand
Catēnā	Chain
Audit	Hears (audio)
Libertas	Liberty

WEEK Eight: VIRTUE and VICE

Gratitude is being thankful for all things and blessing others.

Jealousy is hating others and wanting what they have for yourself.

The Hungry Wolf and the Well-Fed Dog

Milo Winter 1919

READ:

"The Hungry Wolf and the Well-Fed Dog" in English. Use the discussion questions after reading the story aloud.

There was once a Wolf who got very little to eat because the Dogs of the village were so wide awake and watchful. He was really nothing but skin and bones, and it made him very downhearted to think of it.

One night this Wolf happened to fall in with a fine fat House Dog who had wandered a little too far from home. The Wolf would gladly have eaten him then and there, but the House Dog looked strong enough to leave his marks should he try it. So the Wolf spoke very humbly to the Dog, complimenting him on his fine appearance.

"You can be as well-fed as I am if you want to," replied the Dog. "Leave the woods; there you live miserably. Why, you have to fight hard for every bite you get. Follow my example and you will get along beautifully."

"What must I do?" asked the Wolf.

"Hardly anything," answered the House Dog. "Chase people who carry canes, bark at beggars, and fawn on the people of the house. In return you will get tidbits of every kind, chicken bones, choice bits of meat, sugar, cake, and much more besides, not to speak of kind words and caresses."

The Wolf had such a beautiful vision of his coming happiness that he almost wept. But just then he noticed that the hair on the Dog's neck was and the skin was chafed.

"What is that on your neck?"

"Nothing at all," replied the Dog.

"What! Nothing!"

"Oh, just a trifle!"

"But please tell me."

"Perhaps you see the mark of the collar to which my chain is fastened."

"What! A chain!" cried the Wolf. "Don't you go wherever you please?"

"Not always! But what's the difference?" replied the Dog.

"All the difference in the world! I don't care a rap for your feasts and I wouldn't take all the tender young lambs in the world at that price." And away ran the Wolf to the woods.

DISCUSS:

Discuss the story using the discussion questions in the guide and/or questions you come up with.

Discussion Questions:

1. Why do you think the wolf ran away?
2. Who in this story was grateful for what they had? Did anyone show ingratitude?
3. What did the dog think were the most important things in life? What about the wolf?
4. Do you agree more with the dog or the wolf?
5. What do you think are some important things in life worth making sacrifices for? Why?

MEMORIZE:

Memorize the Latin words from the vocabulary bank using one of the review methods below:

- When working with younger children who are not yet reading fluently (4-6), tell them the Latin word, show it to them, and then ask them to create an action, facial expression, or motion to show what the word means. Once they've come up with these, then show them a Latin card, say the word and their task is to quickly do the action, expression or motion they agreed on. As they get the hang of it, go faster and faster. This helps them to associate the correct English meaning to each corresponding Latin term.

- Younger children will also enjoy the game "Canis, Canis, Lupus". This is played by the same rules as "Duck, Duck, Goose". Canis is Latin for dog and Lupus is Latin for wolf.

- When working with older elementary aged children who can read, you can play a card matching game by dividing the students into teams. Feel free to go through several rounds to help them ingrain the words in their memories. Older children (7-11) may also enjoy the more embodied approach described above for younger children.

- The activity Roman Fables in Action is also a good one for both younger and older children. Details for this are in the Year One Teacher's Guide. You can also find them by following the QR code provided at the end of this book.

Latin Skills Group

DISCUSS:

- Ask the children to tell you what they remember from story "The Hungry Wolf and the Well-fed Dog"

- Ask them to put the moral or lesson of the story in their own words. Have the group agree on what this is. Write this down and keep it for future sessions.

- Next, ask the children to help re-write the story in their own words. They should re-tell it in no more than 2-3 sentences. As they experiment aloud with this, you write down what they say, reading it back to them and asking them to help you get the wording right. Write the final summary down and keep it for future sessions.

- Next, tell them that they have all the information they need now to remember and teach the story to someone else. They will do this by memorizing and saying the following:

Lupus et Canis

The Hungry Wolf and the Well-Fed Dog

The story goes that/One day_____ (insert the 2-3 sentence summary they came up with).

The moral is:_____ (insert the moral they came up with)

MEMORIZE:

Memorize the poem in English. If you're ambitions, you can try to memorize the Latin version, too!

Poem in English

The Hungry Wolf and the Well-fed Dog

A hungry wolf met a dog
and commented on his fine appearance.
The dog praised the life of a pet.
The wolf thought it was grand,
until he heard about the chain and collar.

Moral: It is better to be free than to eat a meal in chains.

Poem in Latin

Lupus et Canis

Lupus ēsuriens canem convenit
Et dē speciē bellā sententiam dīcit.
Canis vitam dēliciae laudat.
Lupus putat rem esse grandem,
dum dē catēnā et collāre audit.

Praeceptum: Melius est habēre libertātem quam edere cēnam in catēnīs.

FOLLOW-UP ACTIVITIES:

1. LATIN GAMES
Play some of the Latin games from the Year One Teacher's Guide or QR code at the end of the book.

2. MATH REVIEW GAMES
For children able to do arithmetic, play number knockout. See the Teacher's Guide or QR code for more on the Number Knockout game. For younger children, have them choose a number card and then place the correct number of counters by the number. Or, have younger children review number flash cards as high as they can go. Children can be divided into teams for any of these review games.

3. LANGUAGE ARTS REVIEW GAMES
For younger children, divide into teams to identify letter flash cards. Each time a team member gets a card correct the team gets a point. For older children, play spelling bees. Divide into two teams in front of a chalk or white board. Call out the word and whoever spells it fastest and correctly gets a point for their team.

Latin Skills Group

DISCUSS:

- If you did not complete the moral and story re-telling for "The Hungry Wolf and the Well-Fed Dog" in your last session, start out by completing it now.

- Next, tell them that they have all the information they need now to remember and teach the story to someone else. They will do this by memorizing and saying the following: use the template from Day 2.

- If you did complete it last session, start out by reminding them of the moral and story re-telling they came up with last time and ask them to retell it using the formula above. Use the template from Day 2.

MEMORIZE:
Memorize the poem in English. If you're ambitions, you can try to memorize the Latin version, too!

Use English and Latin poem from Day 2.

Learning Through Art

Week Seven, Day 4 - The Wolf and the Well-Fed Dog

See Learning through Art, Week 8 for instructions.

Latin Skills Group

DISCUSS:

Before starting this activity, create cards with the Latin words in the vocabulary bank for this story. You will find these highlighted in the box below. Create a set of one-sided cards with only the Latin terms; another set of one-sided cards with their English meanings; and a third set of cards with the Latin on front and the English on back. This will allow for different kinds of games and reviews. Introduce and discuss the vocabulary words before reading the fable.

Vocabulary Bank	
Vulpēs	Fox
Dēcidit	Falls down (deciduous)
Puteum	Well
Captus	Trapped (capture)
Caprum	Goat (constellation Capricorn)
Invītat	Invites (invitation)
Intrā	Enter
Bibe	Drink (imbibe)

Vocabulary Bank	
Aquam	Water (aqua, aquarium)
Salit	Jumps
Tergō	Back
Fugit	Escapes (fugitive)

WEEK NINE: VIRTUE and VICE

Self-discipline is being able to do the right thing even when tempted to do something else.

Indiscipline is acting without considering the consequences.

The Fox and the Goat

Milo Winter 1919

READ:

"The Fox and the Goat" in English. Use the discussion questions after reading the story aloud.

A Fox fell into a well, and though it was not very deep, he found that he could not get out again. After he had been in the well a long time, a thirsty Goat came by. The Goat thought the Fox had gone down to drink, and so he asked if the water was good.

"The finest in the whole country," said the crafty Fox, "jump in and try it. There is more than enough for both of us."

The thirsty Goat immediately jumped in and began to drink. The Fox just as quickly jumped on the Goat's back and leaped from the tip of the Goat's horns out of the well.

The foolish Goat now saw what a plight he had got into, and begged the Fox to help him out. But the Fox was already on his way to the woods

"If you had as much sense as you have a beard, old fellow," he said as he ran, "you would have been more cautious about finding a way to get out again before you jumped in."

DISCUSS:

Discuss the story using the discussion questions in the guide and/or questions you come up with.

Discussion Questions:
1.   Do you think the fox did the right thing? Why or why not?
2.   What do you think would have been a better way for the fox to get out? What else could he have done besides trick the goat?
3.   Did the goat do anything right? Did he do anything wrong? Could he have done anything better?

MEMORIZE:

Memorize the Latin words from the vocabulary bank using one of the review methods below:

- When working with younger children who are not yet reading fluently (4-6), tell them the Latin word, show it to them, and then ask them to create an action, facial expression, or motion to show what the word means. Once they've come up with these, then show them a Latin card, say the word and their task is to quickly do the action, expression or motion they agreed on. As they get the hang of it, go faster and faster. This helps them to associate the correct English meaning to each corresponding Latin term.

- Younger children will also enjoy the game "Canis, Canis, Lupus". This is played by the same rules as "Duck, Duck, Goose". Canis is Latin for dog and Lupus is Latin for wolf.

- When working with older elementary aged children who can read, you can play a card matching game by dividing the students into teams. Feel free to go through several rounds to help them ingrain the words in their memories. Older children (7-11) may also enjoy the more embodied approach described above for younger children.

- The activity Roman Fables in Action is also a good one for both younger and older children. Details for this are in the Year One Teacher's Guide. You can also find them by following the QR code provided at the end of this book.

Latin Skills Group

DISCUSS:

- Ask the children to tell you what they remember from story "The Fox and the Goat"

- Ask them to put the moral or lesson of the story in their own words. Have the group agree on what this is. Write this down and keep it for future sessions.

- Next, ask the children to help rewrite the story in their own words. They should re-tell it in no more than 2-3 sentences. As they experiment aloud with this, you write down what they say, reading it back to them and asking them to help you get the wording right. Write the final summary down and keep it for future sessions.

- Next, tell them that they have all the information they need now to remember and teach the story to someone else. They will do this by memorizing and saying the following:

> *Vulpis et Capra*
>
> *The Fox and the Goat*
>
> *The story goes that/One day_____ (insert the 2-3 sentence summary they came up with).*
>
> *The moral is:_____ (insert the moral they came up with)*

MEMORIZE:

Memorize the poem in English. If you're ambitions, you can try to memorize the Latin version, too!

Poem in English

The Fox and the Goat

A fox fell down into a well and was trapped.
So he invited a thirsty goat:
"Enter and drink the finest water!"
But when the goat jumped in the well,
the fox escaped on the goat's back.

Moral: Watch out for dangers when promised a fine reward.

Poem in Latin

Vulpis et Capra

Vulpēs in puteum dēcidit et captus est.
Ita caprum sitiēns invītat:
"Intrā et bibe aquam bellissimam!"
Et ubi caper in puteum salit,
Vulpēs in tergō caprī fugit.

Praeceptum: Cavē perīcula ubi praemium bellum prōmitteris.

FOLLOW-UP ACTIVITIES:

1. LATIN GAMES

Play some of the Latin games from the Year One Teacher's Guide or QR code at the end of the book..

2. MATH REVIEW GAMES

For children able to do arithmetic, play number knockout. See the Teacher's Guide or QR code for more on the Number Knockout game. For younger children, have them choose a number card and then place the correct number of counters by the number. Or, have younger children review number flash cards as high as they can go. Children can be divided into teams for any of these review games.

3. LANGUAGE ARTS REVIEW GAMES

For younger children, divide into teams to identify letter flash cards. Each time a team member gets a card correct the team gets a point. For older children, play spelling bees. Divide into two teams in front of a chalk or white board. Call out the word and whoever spells it fastest and correctly gets a point for their team.

Latin Skills Group

DISCUSS:

- If you did not complete the moral and story re-telling for "The Fox and the Goat" in your last session, start out by completing it now.

- Next, tell them that they have all the information they need now to remember and teach the story to someone else. They will do this by memorizing and saying the following: use the template from Day 2.

- If you did complete it last session, start out by reminding them of the moral and story re-telling they came up with last time and ask them to retell it using the formula above. Use the template from Day 2.

MEMORIZE:

Memorize the poem in English. If you're ambitions, you can try to memorize the Latin version, too!

Use English and Latin poem from Day 2.

Learning Through Art

Week Nine, Day 4 - The Fox and the Goat

See Learning through Art, Week 9 for instructions.

Latin Skills Group

DISCUSS:

Before starting this activity, create cards with the Latin words in the vocabulary bank for this story. You will find these highlighted in the box below. Create a set of one-sided cards with only the Latin terms; another set of one-sided cards with their English meanings; and a third set of cards with the Latin on front and the English on back. This will allow for different kinds of games and reviews. Introduce and discuss the vocabulary words before reading the fable.

Vocabulary Bank	
Vulpēs	Fox
Iuvenis	Young (juvenile)
Leōnem	Lion
Videt	Sees (video)
Arborem	Tree (arboretum)
Cēlat	Hides (conceal)
Provocat	Challenges (provoke)
Faciem	Face (facial)
Verbum	Word (verb, verbal)
Dīcit	Says (dictate, diction

WEEK TEN: VIRTUE and VICE

Heroism is using your strength or knowledge to help and protect others.

Exploitation is when you use someone's weakness to hurt them.

The Fox and the Lion

Milo Winter 1919

READ:

"The Fox and the Lion" in English. Use the discussion questions after reading the story aloud.

A little fox was out playing one day, when a Lion came roaring along.

"Dear me," said the Fox, as he hid behind a tree, "I never saw a Lion before. What a terrible creature! His voice makes me tremble."

The next time the Fox met the Lion he was not so much afraid, but he kept a safe distance and said to himself, "I wish he would not make such a noise!"

The third time they met, the Fox was not frightened at all. He ran up to the Lion, and said, "What are you roaring about?"

And the Lion was so taken by surprise that, without saying a word, he let the Fox walk away.

It would not be safe for little foxes always to follow the example of this one, but it is often true that what our fear makes seem like a lion in the way has no danger in it if we meet it bravely.

DISCUSS:

Discuss the story using the discussion questions in the guide and/or questions you come up with.

Discussion Questions:

1. Why was the fox afraid of the lion at first?
2. Why do you think he became less afraid at the end of the story?
3. Is being afraid ever good for us?
4. Is being afraid ever bad for us? Can it stop us from doing things we ought to do? How?
5. How can you tell the difference between a fear that is protecting you and a fear that is stopping you from doing the right thing?

MEMORIZE:

Memorize the Latin words from the vocabulary bank using one of the review methods below:

- When working with younger children who are not yet reading fluently (4-6), tell them the Latin word, show it to them, and then ask them to create an action, facial expression, or motion to show what the word means. Once they've come up with these, then show them a Latin card, say the word and their task is to quickly do the action, expression or motion they agreed on. As they get the hang of it, go faster and faster. This helps them to associate the correct English meaning to each corresponding Latin term.

- Younger children will also enjoy the game "Canis, Canis, Lupus". This is played by the same rules as "Duck, Duck, Goose". Canis is Latin for dog and Lupus is Latin for wolf.

- When working with older elementary aged children who can read, you can play a card matching game by dividing the students into teams. Feel free to go through several rounds to help them ingrain the words in their memories. Older children (7-11) may also enjoy the more embodied approach described above for younger children.

- The activity Roman Fables in Action is also a good one for both younger and older children. Details for this are in the Year One Teacher's Guide. You can also find them by following the QR code provided at the end of this book.

Latin Skills Group

DISCUSS:

- Ask the children to tell you what they remember from story "The Fox and the Lion"

- Ask them to put the moral or lesson of the story in their own words. Have the group agree on what this is. Write this down and keep it for future sessions.

- Next, ask the children to help rewrite the story in their own words. They should re-tell it in no more than 2-3 sentences. As they experiment aloud with this, you write down what they say, reading it back to them and asking them to help you get the wording right. Write the final summary down and keep it for future sessions.

- Next, tell them that they have all the information they need now to remember and teach the story to someone else. They will do this by memorizing and saying the following:

> *Vulpis et Leo*
>
> *The Fox and the Lion*
>
> *The story goes that/One day_____ (insert the 2-3 sentence summary they came up with).*
>
> *The moral is:_____ (insert the moral they came up with)*

MEMORIZE:

Memorize the poem in English. If you're ambitions, you can try to memorize the Latin version, too!

Poem in English

The Fox and the Lion

When the young fox first saw the roaring lion,
he hid behind a tree.
Next time, he passed by unafraid.
The next time, he challenged the lion to his face.
And the lion? He didn't say a word.

Moral: One who is wise will not be disturbed by the unwise.

Poem in Latin

Vulpis et Leo

Ubi vulpēs iuvenis leōnem fremens prīmum videt,
post aborem sē cēlat.
Deinde impavidē praeterit.
Deinde ad faciem leōnem provocat.
Et leō? Ille verbum nōn dīcit.

Praeceptum: Quī est sapiēns ā imprūdentibus nōn erit perturbātus.

FOLLOW-UP ACTIVITIES:

1. LATIN GAMES

Play some of the Latin games from the Year One Teacher's Guide or QR code at the end of the book. .

2. MATH REVIEW GAMES

For children able to do arithmetic, play number knockout. See the Teacher's Guide or QR code for more on the Number Knockout game. For younger children, have them choose a number card and then place the correct number of counters by the number. Or, have younger children review number flash cards as high as they can go. Children can be divided into teams for any of these review games.

3. LANGUAGE ARTS REVIEW GAMES

For younger children, divide into teams to identify letter flash cards. Each time a team member gets a card correct the team gets a point. For older children, play spelling bees. Divide into two teams in front of a chalk or white board. Call out the word and whoever spells it fastest and correctly gets a point for their team.

Latin Skills Group

DISCUSS:

- If you did not complete the moral and story re-telling for "The Fox and the Lion" in your last session, start out by completing it now.

- Next, tell them that they have all the information they need now to remember and teach the story to someone else. They will do this by memorizing and saying the following: use the template from Day 2.

- If you did complete it last session, start out by reminding them of the moral and story re-telling they came up with last time and ask them to retell it using the formula above. Use the template from Day 2.

MEMORIZE:

Memorize the poem in English. If you're ambitions, you can try to memorize the Latin version, too!

Use English and Latin poem from Day 2.

Learning Through Art

Week Ten, Day 4 - The Fox and the Lion

See Learning through Art, Week 10 for instructions.

Latin Skills Group

DISCUSS:

Before starting this activity, create cards with the Latin words in the vocabulary bank for this story. You will find these highlighted in the box below. Create a set of one-sided cards with only the Latin terms; another set of one-sided cards with their English meanings; and a third set of cards with the Latin on front and the English on back. This will allow for different kinds of games and reviews. Introduce and discuss the vocabulary words before reading the fable.

Vocabulary Bank	
Ursus	Bear (constellation Ursa Major)
Leō	Lion
Haedum	Kid, young goat
Dēsīderant	Want (desire)
Ēsurientēs	Hungry
Pugnant	Fight (pugnacious)
Fessissimī	Very tired (fessī = tired)
Collābuntur	Collapse
Vulpēs	Fox

Vocabulary Bank	
Spectant	Watch (spectator)
Cēnam	Dinner
Capit (Capere)	Takes (capture)

WEEK ELEVEN: VIRTUE and VICE

Generosity is giving whatever you have to others cheerfully.

Miserliness is selfishly keeping everything you have for yourself.

The Bear, the Fox, and the Lion

Milo Winter 1919

READ:
"The Bear, the Fox, and the Lion" in English. Use the discussion questions after reading the story aloud.

Just as a great Bear rushed to seize a stray kid, a Lion leaped from another direction upon the same prey. The two fought furiously for the prize until they had received so many wounds that both sank down unable to continue the battle.

Just then a Fox dashed up, and seizing the kid, made off with it as fast as he could go, while the Lion and the Bear looked on in helpless rage.

"How much better it would have been," they said, "to have shared in a friendly spirit."

DISCUSS:
Discuss the story using the discussion questions in the guide and/or questions you come up with.

Discussion Questions:
1. What happened in this story?
2. How was it that the fox wound up victorious?
3. How could the bear and the lion have changed the outcome?
4. Can you and a friend act out the parts of the bear and lion showing how they could have cooperated and been generous?
5. Are there ever times when it is better to have all/nothing than to only get some? Is it always better to share?

MEMORIZE:

Memorize the Latin words from the vocabulary bank using one of the review methods below:

- When working with younger children who are not yet reading fluently (4-6), tell them the Latin word, show it to them, and then ask them to create an action, facial expression, or motion to show what the word means. Once they've come up with these, then show them a Latin card, say the word and their task is to quickly do the action, expression or motion they agreed on. As they get the hang of it, go faster and faster. This helps them to associate the correct English meaning to each corresponding Latin term.

- Younger children will also enjoy the game "Canis, Canis, Lupus". This is played by the same rules as "Duck, Duck, Goose". Canis is Latin for dog and Lupus is Latin for wolf.

- When working with older elementary aged children who can read, you can play a card matching game by dividing the students into teams. Feel free to go through several rounds to help them ingrain the words in their memories. Older children (7-11) may also enjoy the more embodied approach described above for younger children.

- The activity Roman Fables in Action is also a good one for both younger and older children. Details for this are in the Year One Teacher's Guide. You can also find them by following the QR code provided at the end of this book.

Latin Skills Group

DISCUSS:

- Ask the children to tell you what they remember from the story "The Fox and the Lion".

- Ask them to put the moral or lesson of the story in their own words. Have the group agree on what this is. Write this down and keep it for future sessions.

- Next, ask the children to help rewrite the story in their own words. They should re-tell it in no more than 2-3 sentences. As they experiment aloud with this, you write down what they say, reading it back to them and asking them to help you get the wording right. Write the final summary down and keep it for future sessions.

- Next, tell them that they have all the information they need now to remember and teach the story to someone else. They will do this by memorizing and saying the following:

> *Ursus, Leo, et Vulpis*
>
> *The Bear, the Lion, and the Fox*
>
> *The story goes that/One day _____ (insert the 2-3 sentence summary they came up with).*
>
> *The moral is:_____ (insert the moral they came up with)*

MEMORIZE:

Memorize the poem in English. If you're ambitions, you can try to memorize the Latin version, too!

Poem in English
The Bear, the Lion, and the Fox

A bear and a lion both wanted a young goat,
because they both were hungry.
They fought and fought
until they were very tired and collapsed.
Then they watched as a fox took the meal.

Moral: Those with a shared goal ought to work together.

Poem in Latin
Ursus, Leo, et Vulpis

Ursus et leō uterque haedum dēsīderant,
quod uterque ēsurientēs sunt.
Illī pugnant et pugnant
dum sunt fessissimī et collābuntur.
Tum spectant ut vulpēs cēnam capit.

Praeceptum: Quī cum mēta commūnī simul labōrāre dēbent.

FOLLOW-UP ACTIVITIES:

1. LATIN GAMES

Play some of the Latin games from the Year One Teacher's Guide or QR code at the end of the book..

2. MATH REVIEW GAMES

For children able to do arithmetic, play number knockout. See the Teacher's Guide or QR code for more on the Number Knockout game. For younger children, have them choose a number card and then place the correct number of counters by the number. Or, have younger children review number flash cards as high as they can go. Children can be divided into teams for any of these review games.

3. LANGUAGE ARTS REVIEW GAMES

For younger children, divide into teams to identify letter flash cards. Each time a team member gets a card correct the team gets a point. For older children, play spelling bees. Divide into two teams in front of a chalk or white board. Call out the word and whoever spells it fastest and correctly gets a point for their team.

Latin Skills Group

DISCUSS:

- If you did not complete the moral and story re-telling for "The Bear, the Fox, and the Lion" in your last session, start out by completing it now.

- Next, tell them that they have all the information they need now to remember and teach the story to someone else. They will do this by memorizing and saying the following: use the template from Day 2.

- If you did complete it last session, start out by reminding them of the moral and story re-telling they came up with last time and ask them to retell it using the formula above. Use the template from Day 2.

MEMORIZE:

Memorize the poem in English. If you're ambitions, you can try to memorize the Latin version, too!

Use English and Latin poem from Day 2.

Learning Through Art

Week Eleven, Day 4 - The Bear, the Fox, and the Lion

See Learning through Art, Week 11 for instructions.

Latin Skills Group

DISCUSS:

Before starting this activity, create cards with the Latin words in the vocabulary bank for this story. You will find these highlighted in the box below. Create a set of one-sided cards with only the Latin terms; another set of one-sided cards with their English meanings; and a third set of cards with the Latin on front and the English on back. This will allow for different kinds of games and reviews. Introduce and discuss the vocabulary words before reading the fable.

Vocabulary Bank	
Lupus	Wolf
Caprum	Goat
Saxō	Rock
Cōnspicit	Spies, catches sight of (spectator)
Invītat	Invites (invitation)
Herba	Grass (herb)
Recēns	Fresh (recent)

Vocabulary Bank	
Viridis	Green
Fallitur	Is fooled (fallacy)
Locum	Place (location)
Tūtum	Safe
Relinquit	Leaves (relinquish)

WEEK TWELVE: VIRTUE and VICE

Hospitality is welcoming others into your home and looking to serve them.

Inhospitality is being unwelcoming and rude to others in your home.

The Wolf and the Goat

Milo Winter 1919

READ:

"The Wolf and the Goat" in English. Use the discussion questions after reading the story aloud.

A Wolf saw a Goat feeding at the top of a steep precipice, where he could not reach her.

"My dear friend," said the Wolf, "be careful! I am afraid you will fall and break your neck. Do come down to the meadow, where the grass is fresh and green."

"Are you very hungry?" said the Goat. "And is it your dinner time? And would you like to eat me? I think I will not go down to the meadow today, thank you."

And she capered contentedly about on the edge of the rock, as safe from falling as she was from the greedy Wolf with his false care for her.

DISCUSS:

Discuss the story using the discussion questions in the guide and/or questions you come up with.

Discussion Questions:
1. Was the wolf's concern for the goat genuine? How do you know?
2. Why would the wolf feign care for the goat?
3. How did the goat respond to the wolf's invitation? What do you think would have happened if she had accepted?
4. Was the goat really in danger on the precipice?
5. What if the precipice had really been dangerous for the goat—should she accept the wolf's invitation if she had really been in danger on the mountain?

MEMORIZE:

Memorize the Latin words from the vocabulary bank using one of the review methods below:

*   When working with younger children who are not yet reading fluently (4-6), tell them the Latin word, show it to them, and then ask them to create an action, facial expression, or motion to show what the word means. Once they've come up with these, then show them a Latin card, say the word and their task is to quickly do the action, expression or motion they agreed on. As they get the hang of it, go faster and faster. This helps them to associate the correct English meaning to each corresponding Latin term.

*   Younger children will also enjoy the game "Canis, Canis, Lupus". This is played by the same rules as "Duck, Duck, Goose". Canis is Latin for dog and Lupus is Latin for wolf.

*   When working with older elementary aged children who can read, you can play a card matching game by dividing the students into teams. Feel free to go through several rounds to help them ingrain the words in their memories. Older children (7-11) may also enjoy the more embodied approach described above for younger children.

*   The activity Roman Fables in Action is also a good one for both younger and older children. Details for this are in the Year One Teacher's Guide. You can also find them by following the QR code provided at the end of this book.

Latin Skills Group

DISCUSS:

- Ask the children to tell you what they remember from story "The Wolf and the Goat"

- Ask them to put the moral or lesson of the story in their own words. Have the group agree on what this is. Write this down and keep it for future sessions.

- Next, ask the children to help rewrite the story in their own words. They should re-tell it in no more than 2-3 sentences. As they experiment aloud with this, you write down what they say, reading it back to them and asking them to help you get the wording right. Write the final summary down and keep it for future sessions.

- Next, tell them that they have all the information they need now to remember and teach the story to someone else. They will do this by memorizing and saying the following:

Lupus et Capra

The Wolf and the Goat

The story goes that/One day_____ (insert the 2-3 sentence summary they came up with).

The moral is: _____ (insert the moral they came up with)

MEMORIZE:

Memorize the poem in English. If you're ambitions, you can try to memorize the Latin version, too!

Poem in English

The Wolf and the Goat

A wolf spied a goat on a rock,
so he invited the goat into the meadow,
where there was fresh, green grass.
But the goat was not fooled
and did not leave his safe spot.

Moral: Do not listen to those who promise greener grass.

Poem in Latin

Lupus et Capra

Lupus caprum in saxō cōnspicit,
ita in pratum caprum invītat,
ubi est herba recēns et viridis.
Sed caper nōn fallitur
et locum tūtum nōn relinquit.

Praeceptum: Nōlī auscultāre quibus herbam viridiorem prōmittentibus.

FOLLOW-UP ACTIVITIES:

1. LATIN GAMES

Play some of the Latin games from the Year One Teacher's Guide or QR code at the end of the book.

2. MATH REVIEW GAMES

For children able to do arithmetic, play number knockout. See the Teacher's Guide or QR code for more on the Number Knockout game. For younger children, have them choose a number card and then place the correct number of counters by the number. Or, have younger children review number flash cards as high as they can go. Children can be divided into teams for any of these review games.

3. LANGUAGE ARTS REVIEW GAMES

For younger children, divide into teams to identify letter flash cards. Each time a team member gets a card correct the team gets a point. For older children, play spelling bees. Divide into two teams in front of a chalk or white board. Call out the word and whoever spells it fastest and correctly gets a point for their team.

Latin Skills Group

DISCUSS:

- If you did not complete the moral and story re-telling for "The Wolf and the Goat" in your last session, start out by completing it now.

- Next, tell them that they have all the information they need now to remember and teach the story to someone else. They will do this by memorizing and saying the following: use the template from Day 2.

- If you did complete it last session, start out by reminding them of the moral and story re-telling they came up with last time and ask them to retell it using the formula above. Use the template from Day 2.

MEMORIZE:

Memorize the poem in English. If you're ambitions, you can try to memorize the Latin version, too!

Use English and Latin poem from Day 2.

Learning Through Art

Week Twelve, Day 4 - The Bear, the Fox, and the Lion

See Learning through Art, Week 12 for instructions.

Latin Skills Group

DISCUSS:

Before starting this activity, create cards with the Latin words in the vocabulary bank for this story. You will find these highlighted in the box below. Create a set of one-sided cards with only the Latin terms; another set of one-sided cards with their English meanings; and a third set of cards with the Latin on front and the English on back. This will allow for different kinds of games and reviews. Introduce and discuss the vocabulary words before reading the fable.

Vocabulary Bank	
Viā	Road, way (viaduct)
Fēlēs	Cat (feline)
Vulpēs	Fox
Dolus (dolīs)	Trick, tricks
Canēs	dogs (canine)
Vēnātōris	Hunter
Ūnus	One (uni-)
Vītam	Life (vitality)
Servat	Saves

Vocabulary Bank	
Sequī	To follow (sequence)
Cōnsilium	Idea (counsel)
Optimum	Best (optimal)

WEEK THIRTEEN: VIRTUE and VICE

Industriousness is working hard and well at whatever you have to do.

Laziness is doing work slowly and badly or refusing to work at all.

The Cat and the Fox

Milo Winter 1919

READ:

"The Cat and the Fox" in English. Use the discussion questions after reading the story aloud.

Once a Cat and a Fox were traveling together. As they went along, picking up provisions on the way—a stray mouse here, a fat chicken there—they began an argument to while away the time between bites. And, as usually happens when comrades argue, the talk began to get personal.

"You think you are extremely clever, don't you?" said the Fox. "Do you pretend to know more than I? Why, I know a whole sackful of tricks!"

"Well," retorted the Cat, "I admit I know one trick only, but that one, let me tell you, is worth a thousand of yours!"

Just then, close by, they heard a hunter's horn and the yelping of a pack of hounds. In an instant the Cat was up a tree, hiding among the leaves.

"This is my trick," he called to the Fox. "Now let me see what yours are worth."

But the Fox had so many plans for escape he could not decide which one to try first. He dodged here and there with the hounds at his heels. He doubled on his tracks, he ran at top speed, he entered a dozen burrows,—but all in vain. The hounds caught him, and soon put an end to the boaster and all his tricks.

DISCUSS:

Discuss the story using the discussion questions in the guide and/or questions you come up with.

Discussion Questions:
1. What happened in this story?
2. Why did the fox get caught? What saved the cat?
3. Foxes cannot climb trees like cats. What could the fox have done to save himself?
4. What dangerous situations do we make plans for? (fire drill, etc.)
5. Do you think having that kind of plan is good? What do you think could happen if we didn't make those plans?

MEMORIZE:

Memorize the Latin words from the vocabulary bank using one of the review methods below:

- When working with younger children who are not yet reading fluently (4-6), tell them the Latin word, show it to them, and then ask them to create an action, facial expression, or motion to show what the word means. Once they've come up with these, then show them a Latin card, say the word and their task is to quickly do the action, expression or motion they agreed on. As they get the hang of it, go faster and faster. This helps them to associate the correct English meaning to each corresponding Latin term.

- Younger children will also enjoy the game "Canis, Canis, Lupus". This is played by the same rules as "Duck, Duck, Goose". Canis is Latin for dog and Lupus is Latin for wolf.

- When working with older elementary aged children who can read, you can play a card matching game by dividing the students into teams. Feel free to go through several rounds to help them ingrain the words in their memories. Older children (7-11) may also enjoy the more embodied approach described above for younger children.

- The activity Roman Fables in Action is also a good one for both younger and older children. Details for this are in the Year One Teacher's Guide. You can also find them by following the QR code provided at the end of this book.

Latin Skills Group

DISCUSS:

- Ask the children to tell you what they remember from the story "The Cat and the Fox".

- Ask them to put the moral or lesson of the story in their own words. Have the group agree on what this is. Write this down and keep it for future sessions.

- Next, ask the children to help rewrite the story in their own words. They should re-tell it in no more than 2-3 sentences. As they experiment aloud with this, you write down what they say, reading it back to them and asking them to help you get the wording right. Write the final summary down and keep it for future sessions.

- Next, tell them that they have all the information they need now to remember and teach the story to someone else. They will do this by memorizing and saying the following:

> *Feles et Vulpis*
>
> *The Cat and the Fox*
>
> *The story goes that/One day_____ (insert the 2-3 sentence summary they came up with).*
>
> *The moral is:_____ (insert the moral they came up with)*

MEMORIZE:

Memorize the poem in English. If you're ambitions, you can try to memorize the Latin version, too!

Poem in English
The Cat and the Fox

While on the road, a cat and a fox
argued about cleverness and tricks.
When the hunter's dogs approached,
the cat's one trick saved his life,
but the fox didn't know the best idea.

Moral: Too many good ideas can make you indecisive.

Poem in Latin
Feles et Vulpis

Dum in viā, fēlēs et vulpēs
dē calliditāte et dolīs disputant.
Ubi canēs vēnātōris appropinquant,
ūnus dolus fēlis vītam servat,
sed vulpēs cōnsilium optimum nēscit.

Praeceptum: Plūrima cōnsilia bona facere possunt tē dubius.

FOLLOW-UP ACTIVITIES:

1. LATIN GAMES

Play some of the Latin games from the Year One Teacher's Guide or QR code at the end of the book.

2. MATH REVIEW GAMES

For children able to do arithmetic, play number knockout. See the Teacher's Guide or QR code for more on the Number Knockout game. For younger children, have them choose a number card and then place the correct number of counters by the number. Or, have younger children review number flash cards as high as they can go. Children can be divided into teams for any of these review games.

3. LANGUAGE ARTS REVIEW GAMES

For younger children, divide into teams to identify letter flash cards. Each time a team member gets a card correct the team gets a point. For older children, play spelling bees. Divide into two teams in front of a chalk or white board. Call out the word and whoever spells it fastest and correctly gets a point for their team.

Latin Skills Group

DISCUSS:

- If you did not complete the moral and story re-telling for "The Cat and the Fox" in your last session, start out by completing it now.

- Next, tell them that they have all the information they need now to remember and teach the story to someone else. They will do this by memorizing and saying the following: use the template from Day 2.

- If you did complete it last session, start out by reminding them of the moral and story re-telling they came up with last time and ask them to retell it using the formula above. Use the template from Day 2.

MEMORIZE:

Memorize the poem in English. If you're ambitions, you can try to memorize the Latin version, too!

Use English and Latin poem from Day 2.

Learning Through Art

Week Thirteen, Day 4 - The Cat and the Fox

See Learning through Art, Week 13 for instructions.

Latin Skills Group

DISCUSS:

Before starting this activity, create cards with the Latin words in the vocabulary bank for this story. You will find these highlighted in the box below. Create a set of one-sided cards with only the Latin terms; another set of one-sided cards with their English meanings; and a third set of cards with the Latin on front and the English on back. This will allow for different kinds of games and reviews. Introduce and discuss the vocabulary words before reading the fable.

Vocabulary Bank	
Canis	Dog (Canine)
Gallus	Rooster
Arbore	Tree (arbor, arboretum)
Vulpēs	Fox
Dormiunt	Sleep (dormitory)
Vulpem	Fox
Proximum	Nearby (proximal)
Excitat	Awake (excite)

Vocabulary Bank	
Salūtiōnem	Welcome (salutation)
Accipit	Receive (accept)
Iānuam	Door (January)
Convenit	Meet (convene)

WEEK FOURTEEN: VIRTUE and VICE

Contentment is being happy with what you have.

Envy is wanting what others have so much that you wish them harm.

The Rooster, the Dog, and the Fox

Milo Winter 1919

READ:

"The Rooster, the Dog, and the Fox" in English. Use the discussion questions after reading the story aloud.

A Dog and a Rooster, who were the best of friends, wished very much to see something of the world. So they decided to leave the farmyard and to set out into the world along the road that led to the woods. The two comrades traveled along in the very best of spirits and without meeting any adventure to speak of.

At nightfall the Rooster, looking for a place to roost, as was his custom, spied nearby a hollow tree that he thought would do very nicely for a night's lodging. The Dog could creep inside and the Rooster would fly up on one of the branches. So said, so done, and both slept very comfortably.

With the first glimmer of dawn, the Rooster awoke. For the moment he forgot just where he was. He thought he was still in the farmyard where it had been his duty to arouse the household at daybreak. So standing on tip-toes he flapped his wings and crowed lustily. But instead of awakening the farmer, he awakened a Fox not far off in the woods. The Fox immediately had rosy visions of a very delicious breakfast. Hurrying to the tree where the bird was roosting, he said very politely:

"A hearty welcome to our woods, honored sir. I cannot tell you how glad I am to see you here. I am quite sure we shall become the closest of friends."

"I feel highly flattered, kind sir," replied the Rooster slyly. "If you will please go around to the door of my house at the foot of the tree, my porter will let you in."

The hungry but unsuspecting Fox, went around the tree as he was told, and in a twinkling the Dog had seized him.

DISCUSS:

Discuss the story using the discussion questions in the guide and/or questions you come up with.

Discussion Questions:
1. What happened in this story?
2. The fox spoke very sweetly to the Rooster, but was he genuinely benevolent? How do you know?
3. Do you think the Rooster handled the situation in the right way? Why or why not? What could or should he have done differently?
4. Was anyone in this story benevolent toward someone else?
5. Imagine that the fox really did want to be kind to the Rooster. How could he have gotten the Rooster to trust him?
6. How do you show benevolence to your friends? To strangers?

MEMORIZE:

Memorize the Latin words from the vocabulary bank using one of the review methods below:

- When working with younger children who are not yet reading fluently (4-6), tell them the Latin word, show it to them, and then ask them to create an action, facial expression, or motion to show what the word means. Once they've come up with these, then show them a Latin card, say the word and their task is to quickly do the action, expression or motion they agreed on. As they get the hang of it, go faster and faster. This helps them to associate the correct English meaning to each corresponding Latin term.

- Younger children will also enjoy the game "Canis, Canis, Lupus". This is played by the same rules as "Duck, Duck, Goose". Canis is Latin for dog and Lupus is Latin for wolf.

- When working with older elementary aged children who can read, you can play a card matching game by dividing the students into teams. Feel free to go through several rounds to help them ingrain the words in their memories. Older children (7-11) may also enjoy the more embodied approach described above for younger children.

- The activity Roman Fables in Action is also a good one for both younger and older children. Details for this are in the Year One Teacher's Guide. You can also find them by following the QR code provided at the end of this book.

Latin Skills Group

DISCUSS:

- Ask the children to tell you what they remember from the story "The Rooster, the Dog, and the Fox".

- Ask them to put the moral or lesson of the story in their own words. Have the group agree on what this is. Write this down and keep it for future sessions.

- Next, ask the children to help rewrite the story in their own words. They should re-tell it in no more than 2-3 sentences. As they experiment aloud with this, you write down what they say, reading it back to them and asking them to help you get the wording right. Write the final summary down and keep it for future sessions.

- Next, tell them that they have all the information they need now to remember and teach the story to someone else. They will do this by memorizing and saying the following:

> *Gallus, Canus, et Vulpis*
>
> *The Rooster, the Dog, and the Fox*
>
> *The story goes that/One day_____ (insert the 2-3 sentence summary they came up with).*
>
> *The moral is:_____ (insert the moral they came up with)*

Memorize the poem in English. If you're ambitions, you can try to memorize the Latin version, too!

Poem in English

The Rooster, the Dog, and the Fox

A dog and a rooster slept in a tree one night.
At dawn, the rooster crowed as usual
and awoke a nearby fox.
The fox received a welcome from the rooster,
but at the door he met a hungry dog.

Moral: Those who flatter falsely will be fooled by the flattery of others.

Poem in Latin

Gallus, Canis, et Vulpis

Quādem nocte canis et gallus in arbore dormiunt.
Primā luce, gallus ut solet canit
et vulpem proximum excitat.
Vulpēs ā gallō salūtiōnem accipit,
sed apud iānuam canem ēsuriens convenit.

Praeceptum: Quī falsē blandiuntur ā blanditiā aliōrum fallentur.

FOLLOW-UP ACTIVITIES:

1. LATIN GAMES

Play some of the Latin games from the Year One Teacher's Guide or QR code at the end of the book..

2. MATH REVIEW GAMES

For children able to do arithmetic, play number knockout. See the Teacher's Guide or QR code for more on the Number Knockout game. For younger children, have them choose a number card and then place the correct number of counters by the number. Or, have younger children review number flash cards as high as they can go. Children can be divided into teams for any of these review games.

3. LANGUAGE ARTS REVIEW GAMES

For younger children, divide into teams to identify letter flash cards. Each time a team member gets a card correct the team gets a point. For older children, play spelling bees. Divide into two teams in front of a chalk or white board. Call out the word and whoever spells it fastest and correctly gets a point for their team.

Latin Skills Group

DISCUSS:

- If you did not complete the moral and story re-telling for "The Rooster, the Dog, and the Fox" in your last session, start out by completing it now.

- Next, tell them that they have all the information they need now to remember and teach the story to someone else. They will do this by memorizing and saying the following: use the template from Day 2.

- If you did complete it last session, start out by reminding them of the moral and story re-telling they came up with last time and ask them to retell it using the formula above. Use the template from Day 2.

MEMORIZE:

Memorize the poem in English. If you're ambitions, you can try to memorize the Latin version, too!

Use English and Latin poem from Day 2.

Learning Through Art

Week Fourteen, Day 4 - The Rooster, the Dog, and the Fox

See Learning through Art, Week 14 for instructions.

Latin Skills Group

DISCUSS:

Before starting this activity, create cards with the Latin words in the vocabulary bank for this story. You will find these highlighted in the box below. Create a set of one-sided cards with only the Latin terms; another set of one-sided cards with their English meanings; and a third set of cards with the Latin on front and the English on back. This will allow for different kinds of games and reviews. Introduce and discuss the vocabulary words before reading the fable.

Vocabulary Bank	
Mater	Other (maternal)
Capra	Goat (constellation Capricorn)
Domō	House (domicile)
Ambulat	Walks (ambulance)
Haedum	Kid, young goat
Monet	Warns (admonish)
Hostēs	Enemies (hostile)
Lupus	Wolf
Temptat	Tries (tempt)
Cautus	Cautious
Signum	Sign

Vocabulary Bank	
Petit	Asks for
Pedem	Paw, foot (pedestrian)
Dēmōnstrāre	Show (demonstration)

WEEK FIFTEEN: VIRTUE and VICE

Trustworthiness is being honest and keeping your word.

Untrustworthiness is telling lies, acting sneakily, or breaking promises.

The Wolf and the Young Goat

Milo Winter 1919

READ:

"The Wolf and the Young Goat" in English. Use the discussion questions after reading the story aloud.

Mother Goat was going to market one morning to get provisions for her household, which consisted of but one little Kid and herself.

"Take good care of the house, my son," she said to the Kid, as she carefully latched the door. "Do not let anyone in, unless he gives you this password: 'Down with the Wolf and all his race!'"

Strangely enough, a Wolf was lurking nearby and heard what the Goat had said. So, as soon as Mother Goat was out of sight, up he trotted to the door and knocked.

"Down with the Wolf and all his race," said the Wolf softly.

It was the right password, but when the Kid peeped through a crack in the door and saw the shadowy figure outside, he did not feel at all easy.

"Show me a white paw," he said, "or I won't let you in."

A white paw, of course, is a feature few Wolves can show, and so Master Wolf had to go away as hungry as he had come.

"You can never be too sure," said the Kid, when he saw the Wolf making off to the woods.

DISCUSS:

Discuss the story using the discussion questions in the guide and/or questions you come up with.

Discussion Questions:

1. What happened in this story?
2. Was anyone in this story trustworthy? Untrustworthy?
3. How was the young goat (or kid) supposed to tell the difference between a trustworthy visitor and an untrustworthy one? Did it work?
4. How can you determine who is trustworthy in your life?
5. How can you demonstrate to someone else that you are trustworthy?

MEMORIZE:

Memorize the Latin words from the vocabulary bank using one of the review methods below:

- When working with younger children who are not yet reading fluently (4-6), tell them the Latin word, show it to them, and then ask them to create an action, facial expression, or motion to show what the word means. Once they've come up with these, then show them a Latin card, say the word and their task is to quickly do the action, expression or motion they agreed on. As they get the hang of it, go faster and faster. This helps them to associate the correct English meaning to each corresponding Latin term.

- Younger children will also enjoy the game "Canis, Canis, Lupus". This is played by the same rules as "Duck, Duck, Goose". Canis is Latin for dog and Lupus is Latin for wolf.

- When working with older elementary aged children who can read, you can play a card matching game by dividing the students into teams. Feel free to go through several rounds to help them ingrain the words in their memories. Older children (7-11) may also enjoy the more embodied approach described above for younger children.

- The activity Roman Fables in Action is also a good one for both younger and older children. Details for this are in the Year One Teacher's Guide. You can also find them by following the QR code provided at the end of this book.

FOLLOW-UP ACTIVITIES:

1. LATIN GAMES

Play some of the Latin games from the Year One Teacher's Guide or QR code at the end of the book..

2. MATH REVIEW GAMES

For children able to do arithmetic, play number knockout. See the Teacher's Guide or QR code for more on the Number Knockout game. For younger children, have them choose a number card and then place the correct number of counters by the number. Or, have younger children review number flash cards as high as they can go. Children can be divided into teams for any of these review games.

3. LANGUAGE ARTS REVIEW GAMES

For younger children, divide into teams to identify letter flash cards. Each time a team member gets a card correct the team gets a point. For older children, play spelling bees. Divide into two teams in front of a chalk or white board. Call out the word and whoever spells it fastest and correctly gets a point for their team.

Latin Skills Group

Week Fifteen - The Wolf and the Young Goat
Day 2

DISCUSS:

- Ask the children to tell you what they remember from the story "The Wolf and the Young Goat".

- Ask them to put the moral or lesson of the story in their own words. Have the group agree on what this is. Write this down and keep it for future sessions.

- Next, ask the children to help rewrite the story in their own words. They should re-tell it in no more than 2-3 sentences. As they experiment aloud with this, you write down what they say, reading it back to them and asking them to help you get the wording right. Write the final summary down and keep it for future sessions.

- Next, tell them that they have all the information they need now to remember and teach the story to someone else. They will do this by memorizing and saying the following:

> *Lupus et Haedus*
>
> *The Wolf and the Young Goat*
>
> *The story goes that/One day_____ (insert the 2-3 sentence summary they came up with).*
>
> *The moral is:_____ (insert the moral they came up with)*

MEMORIZE:

Memorize the poem in English. If you're ambitions, you can try to memorize the Latin version, too!

Poem in English

The Wolf and the Young Goat

Before the mother goat walked out of the house,
she warned her kid about enemies.
So when a wolf tried to give the password,
the cautious kid asked for a sign.
But the wolf could not show a white paw.

Moral: Better to be safe than sorry.

Poem in Latin

Lupus et Haedus

Anteā mater capra ē domō ambulat,
illa haedum dē hostēs monet.
Ita ubi lupus tesseram temptat dare,
haedus cautus signum petit.
Sed lupus pedem album dēmōnstrāre nōn potest.

Praeceptum: Melius est tuērī quam paenitēre.

FOLLOW-UP ACTIVITIES:

1. LATIN GAMES

Play some of the Latin games from the Year One Teacher's Guide or QR code at the end of the book..

2. MATH REVIEW GAMES

For children able to do arithmetic, play number knockout. See the Teacher's Guide or QR code for more on the Number Knockout game. For younger children, have them choose a number card and then place the correct number of counters by the number. Or, have younger children review number flash cards as high as they can go. Children can be divided into teams for any of these review games.

3. LANGUAGE ARTS REVIEW GAMES

For younger children, divide into teams to identify letter flash cards. Each time a team member gets a card correct the team gets a point. For older children, play spelling bees. Divide into two teams in front of a chalk or white board. Call out the word and whoever spells it fastest and correctly gets a point for their team.

Latin Skills Group

DISCUSS:

- If you did not complete the moral and story re-telling for "The Wolf and the Young Goat" in your last session, start out by completing it now.

- Next, tell them that they have all the information they need now to remember and teach the story to someone else. They will do this by memorizing and saying the following: use the template from Day 2.

- If you did complete it last session, start out by reminding them of the moral and story re-telling they came up with last time and ask them to retell it using the formula above. Use the template from Day 2.

MEMORIZE:

Memorize the poem in English. If you're ambitions, you can try to memorize the Latin version, too!

Use English and Latin poem from Day 2.

Learning Through Art

Week Fifteen, Day 4 - The Wolf and the Young Goat

See Learning through Art, Week 15 for instructions.

Latin Skills Group

DISCUSS:

Before starting this activity, create cards with the Latin words in the vocabulary bank for this story. You will find these highlighted in the box below. Create a set of one-sided cards with only the Latin terms; another set of one-sided cards with their English meanings; and a third set of cards with the Latin on front and the English on back. This will allow for different kinds of games and reviews. Introduce and discuss the vocabulary words before reading the fable.

Vocabulary Bank	
Omnia	All (omni-)
Animalia	Animals
Viam	Way, path (viaduct)
Magnō	Great (magnitude)
Faciunt	Make (factory)
Leōnī	Lion
Asinus	Donkey
Exclāmat	Yells, shouted (exclamation)
Vertit	Turns
Videt	Sees (video)
Locō	Place (location)
Dēscendit	Stoops, goes down (descend)

WEEK SIXTEEN: VIRTUE and VICE

Gentleness is being tender and kind with your actions and words.

Harshness is treating others with cruelty or severity.

The Lion and the Donkey

Milo Winter 1919

READ:

"The Lion and the Donkey" in English. Use the discussion questions after reading the story aloud.

One day as the Lion walked proudly down a forest aisle, and the animals respectfully made way for him, a Donkey brayed a scornful remark as he passed.

The Lion felt a flash of anger. But when he turned his head and saw who had spoken, he walked quietly on. He would not honor the fool with even so much as a stroke of his claws.

DISCUSS:

Discuss the story using the discussion questions in the guide and/or questions you come up with.

Discussion Questions:

1. Why do you think the Lion chose to ignore the Donkey?
2. Do you think the Lion's response was right?
3. Do you think the Donkey learned any kind of lesson from the Lion's gentle response? Would the Donkey have learned any kind of lesson from an attack by the Lion? Which lesson do you think the Donkey would remember more?
4. Have you ever chosen to be gentle when you would rather attack? What happened?
5. Has anyone ever chosen to be gentle with you? What did you learn from their response?

MEMORIZE:

Memorize the Latin words from the vocabulary bank using one of the review methods below:

- When working with younger children who are not yet reading fluently (4-6), tell them the Latin word, show it to them, and then ask them to create an action, facial expression, or motion to show what the word means. Once they've come up with these, then show them a Latin card, say the word and their task is to quickly do the action, expression or motion they agreed on. As they get the hang of it, go faster and faster. This helps them to associate the correct English meaning to each corresponding Latin term.

- Younger children will also enjoy the game "Canis, Canis, Lupus". This is played by the same rules as "Duck, Duck, Goose". Canis is Latin for dog and Lupus is Latin for wolf.

- When working with older elementary aged children who can read, you can play a card matching game by dividing the students into teams. Feel free to go through several rounds to help them ingrain the words in their memories. Older children (7-11) may also enjoy the more embodied approach described above for younger children.

- The activity Roman Fables in Action is also a good one for both younger and older children. Details for this are in the Year One Teacher's Guide. You can also find them by following the QR code provided at the end of this book.

FOLLOW-UP ACTIVITIES:

1. LATIN GAMES

Play some of the Latin games from the Year One Teacher's Guide or QR code at the end of the book..

2. MATH REVIEW GAMES

For children able to do arithmetic, play number knockout. See the Teacher's Guide or QR code for more on the Number Knockout game. For younger children, have them choose a number card and then place the correct number of counters by the number. Or, have younger children review number flash cards as high as they can go. Children can be divided into teams for any of these review games.

3. LANGUAGE ARTS REVIEW GAMES

For younger children, divide into teams to identify letter flash cards. Each time a team member gets a card correct the team gets a point. For older children, play spelling bees. Divide into two teams in front of a chalk or white board. Call out the word and whoever

Latin Skills Group

DISCUSS:

- Ask the children to tell you what they remember from the story "The Lion and the Donkey".

- Ask them to put the moral or lesson of the story in their own words. Have the group agree on what this is. Write this down and keep it for future sessions.

- Next, ask the children to help rewrite the story in their own words. They should re-tell it in no more than 2-3 sentences. As they experiment aloud with this, you write down what they say, reading it back to them and asking them to help you get the wording right. Write the final summary down and keep it for future sessions.

- Next, tell them that they have all the information they need now to remember and teach the story to someone else. They will do this by memorizing and saying the following:

> *Leo et Asinus*
>
> *The Lion and the Donkey*
>
> *The story goes that/One day_____ (insert the 2-3 sentence summary they came up with).*
>
> *The moral is:_____ (insert the moral they came up with)*

Memorize the poem in English. If you're ambitions, you can try to memorize the Latin version, too!

Poem in English

The Lion and the Donkey

All the animals made a way
for the great and powerful lion.
But the donkey yelled out an insult.
The lion turned and saw the heckler,
but he did not stoop to the fool's level.

Moral: Do not repay insult with insult.

Poem in Latin

Leo et Asinus

Omnia animālia viam faciunt
magnō et validō leōnī.
Sed asinus contumēliam exclāmat.
Leō vertit et convīciātōrem videt,
sed locō tenus stultī nōn dēscendit.

Praeceptum: Nōlī reddere contumēliam contumēliā.

FOLLOW-UP ACTIVITIES:

1. LATIN GAMES

Play some of the Latin games from the Year One Teacher's Guide or QR code at the end of the book. .

2. MATH REVIEW GAMES

For children able to do arithmetic, play number knockout. See the Teacher's Guide or QR code for more on the Number Knockout game. For younger children, have them choose a number card and then place the correct number of counters by the number. Or, have younger children review number flash cards as high as they can go. Children can be divided into teams for any of these review games.

3. LANGUAGE ARTS REVIEW GAMES

For younger children, divide into teams to identify letter flash cards. Each time a team member gets a card correct the team gets a point. For older children, play spelling bees. Divide into two teams in front of a chalk or white board. Call out the word and whoever spells it fastest and correctly gets a point for their team.

Latin Skills Group

DISCUSS:

- If you did not complete the moral and story re-telling for "The Lion and the Donkey" in your last session, start out by completing it now.

- Next, tell them that they have all the information they need now to remember and teach the story to someone else. They will do this by memorizing and saying the following: use the template from Day 2.

- If you did complete it last session, start out by reminding them of the moral and story re-telling they came up with last time and ask them to retell it using the formula above. Use the template from Day 2.

MEMORIZE:

Memorize the poem in English. If you're ambitions, you can try to memorize the Latin version, too!

Use English and Latin poem from Day 2.

Learning Through Art

Week Sixteen, Day 4 - The Lion and the Donkey

See Learning through Art, Week 16 for instructions.

Latin Skills Group

DISCUSS:

Before starting this activity, create cards with the Latin words in the vocabulary bank for this story. You will find these highlighted in the box below. Create a set of one-sided cards with only the Latin terms; another set of one-sided cards with their English meanings; and a third set of cards with the Latin on front and the English on back. This will allow for different kinds of games and reviews. Introduce and discuss the vocabulary words before reading the fable.

Vocabulary Bank	
Fēlēs	Cat (feline)
Avibus	Birds (aviary)
Audit	Hears (audio)
Medicum	Doctor (medic)
Medicāmentum	Medicine, medication

Vocabulary Bank	
Vident	See (video)
Rīdent	Laugh
Invītant	Invite (invitation)

WEEK SEVENTEEN: VIRTUE and VICE

Honesty is telling the truth.

Dishonesty is hiding the truth.

The Cat and the Birds

1905 Conde

READ:

"The Cat and the Birds" in English. Use the discussion questions after reading the story aloud.

A Cat was growing very thin. As you have guessed, he did not get enough to eat. One day he heard that some Birds in the neighborhood were ailing and needed a doctor. So he put on a pair of spectacles, and with a leather box in his hand, knocked at the door of the Bird's home.

The Birds peeped out, and Dr. Cat, with much solicitude, asked how they were. He would be very happy to give them some medicine.

"Tweet, tweet," laughed the Birds. "Very smart, aren't you? We are very well, thank you, and more so, if you only keep away from here."

DISCUSS:
Discuss the story using the discussion questions in the guide and/or questions you come up with.

Discussion Questions:
1. What happened in this story?
2. Was the cat being honest with the birds?
3. How did the birds respond to the cat's dishonesty? Do you think that they responded well or poorly?
4. Do you think the cat could have gotten food for himself without being dishonest? How? 5. Have you ever seen someone be dishonest and get what they want from it? How did that make you feel? Have you ever been dishonest and gotten away with it? How did that make you feel? Is it ever okay to be dishonest to get something you want or need?

MEMORIZE:

Memorize the Latin words from the vocabulary bank using one of the review methods below:

- When working with younger children who are not yet reading fluently (4-6), tell them the Latin word, show it to them, and then ask them to create an action, facial expression, or motion to show what the word means. Once they've come up with these, then show them a Latin card, say the word and their task is to quickly do the action, expression or motion they agreed on. As they get the hang of it, go faster and faster. This helps them to associate the correct English meaning to each corresponding Latin term.

- Younger children will also enjoy the game "Canis, Canis, Lupus". This is played by the same rules as "Duck, Duck, Goose". Canis is Latin for dog and Lupus is Latin for wolf.

- When working with older elementary aged children who can read, you can play a card matching game by dividing the students into teams. Feel free to go through several rounds to help them ingrain the words in their memories. Older children (7-11) may also enjoy the more embodied approach described above for younger children.

- The activity Roman Fables in Action is also a good one for both younger and older children. Details for this are in the Year One Teacher's Guide. You can also find them by following the QR code provided at the end of this book.

FOLLOW-UP ACTIVITIES:

1. LATIN GAMES

Play some of the Latin games from the Year One Teacher's Guide or QR code at the end of the book. .

2. MATH REVIEW GAMES

For children able to do arithmetic, play number knockout. See the Teacher's Guide or QR code for more on the Number Knockout game. For younger children, have them choose a number card and then place the correct number of counters by the number. Or, have younger children review number flash cards as high as they can go. Children can be divided into teams for any of these review games.

3. LANGUAGE ARTS REVIEW GAMES

For younger children, divide into teams to identify letter flash cards. Each time a team member gets a card correct the team gets a point. For older children, play spelling bees. Divide into two teams in front of a chalk or white board. Call out the word and whoever spells it fastest and correctly gets a point for their team.

Latin Skills Group

DISCUSS:

- Ask the children to tell you what they remember from the story "The Cat and the Birds".

- Ask them to put the moral or lesson of the story in their own words. Have the group agree on what this is. Write this down and keep it for future sessions.

- Next, ask the children to help rewrite the story in their own words. They should re-tell it in no more than 2-3 sentences. As they experiment aloud with this, you write down what they say, reading it back to them and asking them to help you get the wording right. Write the final summary down and keep it for future sessions.

- Next, tell them that they have all the information they need now to remember and teach the story to someone else. They will do this by memorizing and saying the following:

Feles et Aves

The Cat and the Birds

The story goes that/One day_____ (insert the 2-3 sentence summary they came up with).

The moral is:_____ (insert the moral they came up with)

MEMORIZE:

Memorize the poem in English. If you're ambitions, you can try to memorize the Latin version, too!

Poem in English

The Cat and the Birds

A hungry cat heard there were sick birds,
so he disguised himself as a doctor.
The cat offered the birds medicine,
but they saw him and laughed
and did not invite him inside.

Moral: Do not trust a person who takes advantage of the vulnerable.

Poem in Latin

Feles et Aves

Fēlēs ēsuriens dē avibus aegrīs audit,
ita sē medicum dissimulat.
Fēlēs medicāmentum avibus offert,
sed eum vident et rīdent
et eum intus nōn invītant.

Praeceptum: Nōlī crēdere hominī quī vulnerābilibus abūtitur.

·

FOLLOW-UP ACTIVITIES:

1. LATIN GAMES

Play some of the Latin games from the Year One Teacher's Guide or QR code at the end of the book. .

2. MATH REVIEW GAMES

For children able to do arithmetic, play number knockout. See the Teacher's Guide or QR code for more on the Number Knockout game. For younger children, have them choose a number card and then place the correct number of counters by the number. Or, have younger children review number flash cards as high as they can go. Children can be divided into teams for any of these review games.

3. LANGUAGE ARTS REVIEW GAMES

For younger children, divide into teams to identify letter flash cards. Each time a team member gets a card correct the team gets a point. For older children, play spelling bees. Divide into two teams in front of a chalk or white board. Call out the word and whoever spells it fastest and correctly gets a point for their team.

Latin Skills Group

DISCUSS:

- If you did not complete the moral and story re-telling for "The Cat and the Birds" in your last session, start out by completing it now.

- Next, tell them that they have all the information they need now to remember and teach the story to someone else. They will do this by memorizing and saying the following: use the template from Day 2.

- If you did complete it last session, start out by reminding them of the moral and story re-telling they came up with last time and ask them to retell it using the formula above. Use the template from Day 2.

MEMORIZE:

Memorize the poem in English. If you're ambitions, you can try to memorize the Latin version, too!

Use English and Latin poem from Day 2.

Learning Through Art

Week Seventeen, Day 4 - The Cat and the Birds

See Learning through Art, Week 17 for instructions.

Latin Skills Group

DISCUSS:

Before starting this activity, create cards with the Latin words in the vocabulary bank for this story. You will find these highlighted in the box below. Create a set of one-sided cards with only the Latin terms; another set of one-sided cards with their English meanings; and a third set of cards with the Latin on front and the English on back. This will allow for different kinds of games and reviews. Introduce and discuss the vocabulary words before reading the fable.

Vocabulary Bank	
Asinus	Donkey
Pelle	Skin (pelt)
Leōnis	Lion (constellation Leo)
Parva	Small
Animālia	Animals
Terret	Scares (terrified)
Vulpem	Fox
Fallere	Fool, trick, deceive (fallacy)
Vōx (voc-)	Voice (vocal)
Speciem	Appearance (species)
Adaequat	Matches, equals
Fremit	Roars

WEEK EIGHTEEN: VIRTUE and VICE

Fortitude is staying strong under pressure.

Faint-heartedness is giving up easily.

The Donkey in a Lion's Skin

Milo Winter 1919

READ:

"The Donkey in a Lion's Skin" in English. Use the discussion questions after reading the story aloud.

A Donkey once put on a Lion's skin which some hunters had spread out to dry. It did not fit the Donkey very well, but he found that in it he could frighten all the timid, foolish little animals, so he amused himself by chasing them about.

By and by he met a Fox, and tried to frighten him by roaring.

"My dear Donkey," said the wise Fox, "you are braying, and not roaring. I might, perhaps, have been frightened by your looks, if you had not tried to roar; but I know your voice too well to mistake you for a Lion."

DISCUSS:

Discuss the story using the discussion questions in the guide and/or questions you come up with.

Discussion Questions:
1. Why do you think the donkey put on the lion skin to begin with?
2. The story says that the donkey entertained himself by frightening others. Was this a kind thing to do? How could the donkey have entertained himself with the skin in a kinder way?
3. How was the donkey's trick ultimately discovered?
4. What do you think the donkey learned from this experience? What do you think the frightened animals might have learned? The fox?

MEMORIZE:

Memorize the Latin words from the vocabulary bank using one of the review methods below:

- When working with younger children who are not yet reading fluently (4-6), tell them the Latin word, show it to them, and then ask them to create an action, facial expression, or motion to show what the word means. Once they've come up with these, then show them a Latin card, say the word and their task is to quickly do the action, expression or motion they agreed on. As they get the hang of it, go faster and faster. This helps them to associate the correct English meaning to each corresponding Latin term.

- Younger children will also enjoy the game "Canis, Canis, Lupus". This is played by the same rules as "Duck, Duck, Goose". Canis is Latin for dog and Lupus is Latin for wolf.

- When working with older elementary aged children who can read, you can play a card matching game by dividing the students into teams. Feel free to go through several rounds to help them ingrain the words in their memories. Older children (7-11) may also enjoy the more embodied approach described above for younger children.

- The activity Roman Fables in Action is also a good one for both younger and older children. Details for this are in the Year One Teacher's Guide. You can also find them by following the QR code provided at the end of this book.

FOLLOW-UP ACTIVITIES:

1. LATIN GAMES

Play some of the Latin games from the Year One Teacher's Guide or QR code at the end of the book. .

2. MATH REVIEW GAMES

For children able to do arithmetic, play number knockout. See the Teacher's Guide or QR code for more on the Number Knockout game. For younger children, have them choose a number card and then place the correct number of counters by the number. Or, have younger children review number flash cards as high as they can go. Children can be divided into teams for any of these review games.

3. LANGUAGE ARTS REVIEW GAMES

For younger children, divide into teams to identify letter flash cards. Each time a team member gets a card correct the team gets a point. For older children, play spelling bees. Divide into two teams in front of a chalk or white board. Call out the word and whoever spells it fastest and correctly gets a point for their team.

Latin Skills Group

DISCUSS:

- Ask the children to tell you what they remember from the story "The Donkey in the a Lion's Skin".

- Ask them to put the moral or lesson of the story in their own words. Have the group agree on what this is. Write this down and keep it for future sessions.

- Next, ask the children to help rewrite the story in their own words. They should re-tell it in no more than 2-3 sentences. As they experiment aloud with this, you write down what they say, reading it back to them and asking them to help you get the wording right. Write the final summary down and keep it for future sessions.

- Next, tell them that they have all the information they need now to remember and teach the story to someone else. They will do this by memorizing and saying the following:

Asinus in Pelle Lionis

The Donkey in a Lion's Skin

The story goes that/One day_____ (insert the 2-3 sentence summary they came up with).

The moral is:_____ (insert the moral they came up with)

MEMORIZE:

Memorize the poem in English. If you're ambitions, you can try to memorize the Latin version, too!

Poem in English

The Donkey in a Lion's Skin

A donkey dressed in a lion's skin,
and he scared the little animals.
But he could not fool the fox
because his voice did not match his appearance.
A donkey does not roar like a lion.

Moral: Listen for the truth, because appearances often deceive.

Poem in Latin

Asinus in belle leonis

Asinus in pelle leōnis sē induit,
et parva animālia terret.
Sed vulpem fallere nōn potest
quod vōx speciem nōn adaequat.
Asinus nōn fremit sicut leō.

Praeceptum: Ausculta vēritātem, quod speciēs saepe dēcipit.

FOLLOW-UP ACTIVITIES:

1. LATIN GAMES

Play some of the Latin games from the Year One Teacher's Guide or QR code at the end of the book. .

2. MATH REVIEW GAMES

For children able to do arithmetic, play number knockout. See the Teacher's Guide or QR code for more on the Number Knockout game. For younger children, have them choose a number card and then place the correct number of counters by the number. Or, have younger children review number flash cards as high as they can go. Children can be divided into teams for any of these review games.

3. LANGUAGE ARTS REVIEW GAMES

For younger children, divide into teams to identify letter flash cards. Each time a team member gets a card correct the team gets a point. For older children, play spelling bees. Divide into two teams in front of a chalk or white board. Call out the word and whoever spells it fastest and correctly gets a point for their team.

Latin Skills Group

DISCUSS:

- If you did not complete the moral and story re-telling for "The Donkey in a Lion's Skin" in your last session, start out by completing it now.

- Next, tell them that they have all the information they need now to remember and teach the story to someone else. They will do this by memorizing and saying the following:

- If you did complete it last session, start out by reminding them of the moral and story re telling they came up with last time and ask them to retell it using the formula above.

MEMORIZE:

Memorize the poem in English. If you're ambitions, you can try to memorize the Latin version, too!

Use English and Latin poem from Day 2.

Learning Through Art

Week Eighteen, Day 4 - The Donkey in a Lion's Skin

See Learning through Art, Week 18 for instructions.

Latin Skills Group

DISCUSS:

Before starting this activity, create cards with the Latin words in the vocabulary bank for this story. You will find these highlighted in the box below. Create a set of one-sided cards with only the Latin terms; another set of one-sided cards with their English meanings; and a third set of cards with the Latin on front and the English on back. This will allow for different kinds of games and reviews. Introduce and discuss the vocabulary words before reading the fable.

Vocabulary Bank	
Mūrēs	Mice
Consilium	Plan (counsel
Pōnāmus (pos-)	Put (position)
Tintinnābulum	Small bell (tinnitus)
Fēle	Cat (feline)
Tūtī	Safe

Vocabulary Bank	
Nēmō	No one
Facere (faciō)	Do, make (facilitate)
Nihil	Nothing (ex nihilo)
Mūtat	Changes (mutate)

WEEK NINETEEN: VIRTUE and VICE

Courage is doing the right thing even when it's scary.

Cowardice is letting fear control your actions.

The Cat and the Mice

Gustave Doré's illustration of La Fontaine's fable, c. 1868

READ:

"The Cat and the Mice" in English. Use the discussion questions after reading the story aloud.

Some little Mice, who lived in the walls of a house, met together one night, to talk of the wicked Cat and to consider what could be done to get rid of her. The head Mice were Brown-back, Gray-ear, and White-whisker.

"There is no comfort in the house," said Brown-back. "If I but step into the pantry to pick up a few crumbs, down comes the Cat, and I have hardly time to run to my nest again."

"What can we do?" asked Gray-ear. "Shall we all run at her at once and bite her, and frighten her away?"

"No," said White-whisker; "she is so bold we could not frighten her. I have thought of something better than that. Let us hang a bell around her neck. Then, if she moves, the bell will ring, and we shall hear it, and have time to run away."

"O yes! yes!" cried all the Mice. "That is a capital idea. We will bell the Cat! Hurrah! hurrah! No more fear of the Cat!" and they danced in glee.

When their glee had subsided a little, Brown-back asked, "But who will hang the bell around her neck?"

No one answered. "Will you?" he asked of White-whisker.

"I don't think I can," replied White-whisker; "I am lame, you know. It needs someone who can move quickly."

"Will you, Gray-ear?" said Brown-back.

"Excuse me," answered Gray-ear; "I have not been well since that time when I was almost caught in the trap."

"Who will bell the Cat, then?" said Brown-back. "If it is to be done, someone must do it."

Not a sound was heard, and one by one the little Mice stole away to their holes, no better off than they were before.

DISCUSS:
Discuss the story using the discussion questions in the guide and/or questions you come up with.

Discussion Questions:
1. What problem were the mice facing?
2. What plan did the mice devise to solve the problem?
3. Do you think their plan was a good one? What was the one difficulty with their plan? Can you think of any other difficulties the mice didn't consider?
4. Did any of the mice in the story exhibit courage?
5. Imagine that there was one courageous mouse in the council. I, your teacher, will re-read the story until Brown-back asks "Who will bell the Cat, then? If it is to be done, someone must do it." In your notebooks, you will rewrite the rest of the story adding in the courageous mouse. Tell me what happens after Brown-back asks his question. What will your courageous mouse say? What will he do? How will the story end?

MEMORIZE:

Memorize the Latin words from the vocabulary bank using one of the review methods below:

- When working with younger children who are not yet reading fluently (4-6), tell them the Latin word, show it to them, and then ask them to create an action, facial expression, or motion to show what the word means. Once they've come up with these, then show them a Latin card, say the word and their task is to quickly do the action, expression or motion they agreed on. As they get the hang of it, go faster and faster. This helps them to associate the correct English meaning to each corresponding Latin term.

- Younger children will also enjoy the game "Canis, Canis, Lupus". This is played by the same rules as "Duck, Duck, Goose". Canis is Latin for dog and Lupus is Latin for wolf.

- When working with older elementary aged children who can read, you can play a card matching game by dividing the students into teams. Feel free to go through several rounds to help them ingrain the words in their memories. Older children (7-11) may also enjoy the more embodied approach described above for younger children.

- The activity Roman Fables in Action is also a good one for both younger and older children. Details for this are in the Year One Teacher's Guide. You can also find them by following the QR code provided at the end of this book.

FOLLOW-UP ACTIVITIES:

1. LATIN GAMES

Play some of the Latin games from the Year One Teacher's Guide or QR code at the end of the book. .

2. MATH REVIEW GAMES

For children able to do arithmetic, play number knockout. See the Teacher's Guide or QR code for more on the Number Knockout game. For younger children, have them choose a number card and then place the correct number of counters by the number. Or, have younger children review number flash cards as high as they can go. Children can be divided into teams for any of these review games.

3. LANGUAGE ARTS REVIEW GAMES

For younger children, divide into teams to identify letter flash cards. Each time a team member gets a card correct the team gets a point. For older children, play spelling bees. Divide into two teams in front of a chalk or white board. Call out the word and whoever spells it fastest and correctly gets a point for their team.

Latin Skills Group

DISCUSS:

- Ask the children to tell you what they remember from the story "The Cat and the Mice".

- Ask them to put the moral or lesson of the story in their own words. Have the group agree on what this is. Write this down and keep it for future sessions.

- Next, ask the children to help rewrite the story in their own words. They should re-tell it in no more than 2-3 sentences. As they experiment aloud with this, you write down what they say, reading it back to them and asking them to help you get the wording right. Write the final summary down and keep it for future sessions.

- Next, tell them that they have all the information they need now to remember and teach the story to someone else. They will do this by memorizing and saying the following:

> *Feles et Mures*
>
> *The Cat and the Mice*
>
> *The story goes that/One day_____ (insert the 2-3 sentence summary they came up with).*
>
> *The moral is:_____ (insert the moral they came up with)*

MEMORIZE:

Memorize the poem in English. If you're ambitions, you can try to memorize the Latin version, too!

Poem in English

The Cat and the Mice

The mice had a plan:
"Let's put a bell on the cat,
so we will be safe!"
But no one wanted to do it,
and so nothing changed.

Moral: A bold plan seems good, but the deed itself is another matter.

Poem in Latin

Feles et Mures

Mūrēs cōnsilium capiunt:
"Pōnāmus tintinnābulum in fēle
ita tūtī erimus!"
Sed nēmō rem facere vult,
itaque nihil mūtat.

Praeceptum: Cōnsilium audax vidētur bonum, factum ipsum est aliam rem.

FOLLOW-UP ACTIVITIES:

1. LATIN GAMES

Play some of the Latin games from the Year One Teacher's Guide or QR code at the end of the book. .

2. MATH REVIEW GAMES

For children able to do arithmetic, play number knockout. See the Teacher's Guide or QR code for more on the Number Knockout game. For younger children, have them choose a number card and then place the correct number of counters by the number. Or, have younger children review number flash cards as high as they can go. Children can be divided into teams for any of these review games.

3. LANGUAGE ARTS REVIEW GAMES

For younger children, divide into teams to identify letter flash cards. Each time a team member gets a card correct the team gets a point. For older children, play spelling bees. Divide into two teams in front of a chalk or white board. Call out the word and whoever

Latin Skills Group

DISCUSS:

- If you did not complete the moral and story re-telling for "The Cat and the Mice" in your last session, start out by completing it now.

- Next, tell them that they have all the information they need now to remember and teach the story to someone else. They will do this by memorizing and saying the following:

- If you did complete it last session, start out by reminding them of the moral and story re telling they came up with last time and ask them to retell it using the formula above.

MEMORIZE:

Memorize the poem in English. If you're ambitions, you can try to memorize the Latin version, too!

Use English and Latin poem from Day 2.

Learning Through Art

Week Nineteen, Day 4 - The Cat and the Mice

See Learning through Art, Week 19 for instructions.

Latin Skills Group

DISCUSS:

Before starting this activity, create cards with the Latin words in the vocabulary bank for this story. You will find these highlighted in the box below. Create a set of one-sided cards with only the Latin terms; another set of one-sided cards with their English meanings; and a third set of cards with the Latin on front and the English on back. This will allow for different kinds of games and reviews. Introduce and discuss the vocabulary words before reading the fable.

Vocabulary Bank	
Asinus	Donkey
Canī (canis)	Dog (canine)
Dominī	Master (dominion)
Domum	House (domicile, domestic)
Intrat	Enters
Agere	Act, do, carry on
Magnās	Great, large (magnificent)
Turbās	Mess, chaos (turbulent)
Servī	Servants
Pūniunt	Punish (punitive)

WEEK TWENTY: VIRTUE and VICE

Joy is enthusiastically enjoying your blessings.

Despair is giving up hope when things get hard.

The Donkey and the Dog

Milo Winter 1919

READ:

"The Donkey and the Dog" in English. Use the discussion questions after reading the story aloud.

There was once a Donkey whose Master also owned a Lap Dog. This Dog was a favorite and received many a pat and kind words from his Master, as well as choice bits from his plate. Every day the Dog would run to meet the Master, frisking playfully about and leaping up to lick his hands and face.

All this the Donkey saw with much discontent. Though he was well fed, he had much work to do; besides, the Master hardly ever took any notice of him.

Now the jealous Donkey got it into his silly head that all he had to do to win his Master's favor was to act like the Dog. So one day he left his stable and clattered eagerly into the house.

Finding his Master seated at the dinner table, he kicked up his heels and, with a loud bray, pranced giddily around the table, upsetting it as he did so. Then he planted his forefeet on his Master's knees and rolled out his tongue to lick the Master's face, as he had seen the Dog do. But his weight upset the chair, and Donkey and the man rolled over together in the pile of broken dishes from the table.

The Master was much alarmed at the strange behavior of the Donkey, and calling for help, soon attracted the attention of the servants. When they saw the danger the Master was in from the clumsy beast, they set upon the Donkey and drove him with kicks and blows back to the stable. There they left him to mourn the foolishness that had brought him nothing but a sound beating.

DISCUSS:

Discuss the story using the discussion questions in the guide and/or questions you come up with.

Discussion Questions:

1. Why was the Donkey upset at the beginning of the story? What plan did he devise? Was that plan successful?
2. What virtue or vice would you say best describes the donkey at the beginning of the story? What virtue or vice does he display in the middle? At the end?
3. What do you think the donkey learned through his actions? How do you think the donkey should have handled his feelings of jealousy?
4. Have you ever felt jealous of someone else? What do you think is the right way to handle our feelings of jealousy?
5. Was the dog's behavior wrong for the dog? Why was the donkey punished for the same behavior as the dog? Was what the donkey did wrong?
6. Have you ever tried, like the donkey, to make yourself more like someone else? Is doing that always a bad thing? How can you tell the difference between trying to be like someone else in a good way and trying to be like someone else in a bad way?

MEMORIZE:

Memorize the Latin words from the vocabulary bank using one of the review methods below:

- When working with younger children who are not yet reading fluently (4-6), tell them the Latin word, show it to them, and then ask them to create an action, facial expression, or motion to show what the word means. Once they've come up with these, then show them a Latin card, say the word and their task is to quickly do the action, expression or motion they agreed on. As they get the hang of it, go faster and faster. This helps them to associate the correct English meaning to each corresponding Latin term.

- Younger children will also enjoy the game "Canis, Canis, Lupus". This is played by the same rules as "Duck, Duck, Goose". Canis is Latin for dog and Lupus is Latin for wolf.

- When working with older elementary aged children who can read, you can play a card matching game by dividing the students into teams. Feel free to go through several rounds to help them ingrain the words in their memories. Older children (7-11) may also enjoy the more embodied approach described above for younger children.

- The activity Roman Fables in Action is also a good one for both younger and older children. Details for this are in the Year One Teacher's Guide. You can also find them by following the QR code provided at the end of this book.

FOLLOW-UP ACTIVITIES:

1. LATIN GAMES

Play some of the Latin games from the Year One Teacher's Guide or QR code at the end of this book. .

2. MATH REVIEW GAMES

For children able to do arithmetic, play number knockout. See the Teacher's Guide or QR code for more on the Number Knockout game. For younger children, have them choose a number card and then place the correct number of counters by the number. Or, have younger children review number flash cards as high as they can go. Children can be divided into teams for any of these review games.

3. LANGUAGE ARTS REVIEW GAMES

For younger children, divide into teams to identify letter flash cards. Each time a team member gets a card correct the team gets a point. For older children, play spelling bees. Divide into two teams in front of a chalk or white board. Call out the word and whoever

Latin Skills Group

DISCUSS:

- Ask the children to tell you what they remember from the story "The Donkey and the Dog".

- Ask them to put the moral or lesson of the story in their own words. Have the group agree on what this is. Write this down and keep it for future sessions.

- Next, ask the children to help rewrite the story in their own words. They should re-tell it in no more than 2-3 sentences. As they experiment aloud with this, you write down what they say, reading it back to them and asking them to help you get the wording right. Write the final summary down and keep it for future sessions.

- Next, tell them that they have all the information they need now to remember and teach the story to someone else. They will do this by memorizing and saying the following:

> *Asinus et Canis*
>
> *The Donkey and the Dog*
>
> *The story goes that/One day_____ (insert the 2-3 sentence summary they came up with).*
>
> *The moral is:_____ (insert the moral they came up with)*

MEMORIZE:

Memorize the poem in English. If you're ambitions, you can try to memorize the Latin version, too!

The Donkey and the Dog

A donkey envied his master's dog,
so he entered the house
and started to behave like a dog.
But he made a great mess,
and the master's servants punished him.

Moral: Discontent only leads to greater trouble.

Asinus et Canis

Asinus canī dominī invīdet,
ita domum intrat
et incipit se gerere sicut canis.
Sed magnās turbās concit.
et servī dominī eum pūniunt.

Praeceptum: Offēnsiōnēs ad maius malum sōlum dūxērunt.

Nyansa Classical Community

Nyansa Classical Community provides classical, Christian curricula and programming designed to connect with and draw students from diverse backgrounds into the beauty of classical literature and the Great Conversation.

- Our curricula and programming:

- Cultivating the poetic and moral imaginations

- Deepen delight and enjoyment of classical literature, language, and art

- Tell classic stories using culturally and ethically diverse images that resonate with young people from a variety of backgrounds

- Encourage students to cultivate truth, goodness, and beauty

For more information, please go to nyansaclassicalcommunity.org.

Nyansa Materials

This workbook is intended to be used alongside our Year One Elementary Curricula. This book should be purchased with Nyansa Year One Latin Workbook.

To order additional materials please go to:
www.nyansaclassicalcommunity.org

Appendix

To access our Latin closing games, training videos, and other resources, scan the QR code below. For more training and information, you can buy our Year One Teacher's Guide online. You can also contact us at nyansa.assistant@gmail.com for access to our training materials.